An Empathy :::: Support Services publication

Alcoholism And Beyond Includes 'The Road To Becoming An Alcoholic And The Way Back', And 'The Book Revisited'

GARY WESTWELL

ISBN No. 1-905546-15-7
978-1-905546-15-2

Published by Write Books CPR LTD
Units 9/ 10 Ferrybridge Workspace,
Pontefract Road, Ferrybridge,
West Yorkshire

WF11 8PL

---oOo---

THE AUTHOR

GARY, JOHN WESTWELL

---oOo---

---oOo---

This is for my dad George Westwell

For Maureen my wife,
and my children Sam and Lydia

---oOo---

People can work very hard climbing the ladder
of success only to discover its leaning against
the wrong wall : Stephen R. Covey

You can spend years building up the respect
and trust of people only to blow it by having
one more drink and pissing it against the
wrong wall: Gary J. Westwell

<u>Contents</u>

ACKNOWLEDGEMENTS

This is the second book I have managed to write about alcohol and its effects on peoples lives. Managing to string a few words together was never easy when I was not drinking and even harder when I was. Thankfully the completion of this second book is down to the unstinting support of a very special group of people.

Heading the list is my wife, Maureen who has not only managed to hold down a job, look after her family and help me with counselling but keep me together, and support the writing all the way. Thanks for putting up with my funny ways for the last six months, in fact most of the time I have known you. I know I'm still a stubborn old git and far more but I didn't want to swear so soon into the book. There's one thing though, I'm still not drinking and aim to continue this way.

A big thanks too goes to the many people whether suffering from alcoholism themselves or their families witnessing it, for their help and advice. Thanks must go to my friend Carolyn, who had the patience to read through my original book and point out all the spelling mistakes. She has also corrected these additions.

My indefatigable son who has very patiently battled with the seemingly illogical way my computer tends to operate I also thank, particularly since he bought a laptop with his birthday money. In addition of course my mum and my daughter, Lydia who I feel always believed I would 'come right' in the end, and have helped me with their very searching but true comments about me. Lydia is a much more mature person nowadays and this is seen in the chapter she wrote herself.

I would also like to thank Eric and Margaret Biddulph, Alistair Megahy, Matthew Holland Elaine Peaker, Louanne Craven and the team at 'Womanspace' for all their help, and support. Last, but not least, thanks go to the support of the National Lottery through Awards For All for stumping up the money to get this thing printed.

No thanks go to the bloke who beat me senseless one Christmas when yet again I was worse for wear. As any alcoholic will tell you waking up covered in bruises is not unusual, but not nice.

Great care has been taken to ensure that the

information in this book is accurate, but if errors remain then the responsibility is mine. Please let me know if you spot any. I can be contacted at: Gary @ empathy support services or telephone 01484 469030

<u>EMPATHY</u>

Empathy is the ability to experience, and respond to, another person's feelings. Empathy is more than just awareness of another person's emotions. It's feeling those emotions within and expressing your feelings in a heartfelt way. Empathy requires the cognitive ability to understand another person's feelings and thoughts, and the emotion to actually feel them. Some scientists believe that empathy also includes the ability to communicate that understanding to another person.

To some extent, our ability to be empathetic is genetic, inherited over generations. There is a survival value to the human species to be able to know what another human is experiencing. But, empathy can also be taught. Studies of adults have shown that those who are more empathic tend to be happier. For one thing, they're motivated to do things for others and helping others increases their own happiness. On the opposite end of the spectrum, people who remain preoccupied with themselves tend to be unhappy.

Empathy increases with age. In general, adolescents are capable of, and show, more empathy than toddlers while adults are capable of, and show, more empathy than adolescents. In addition, woman tend to be more empathic than men.

When we experience empathy, three things happen. First we recognise a person's emotional state. Secondly, we connect to that state and actually experience it ourselves. And third, we act on it. We show our feelings to the other person or talk with that person in depth about what he or she is experiencing.

You can become more empathic by :

- Increasing your awareness of your inner emotional states. It's easier to recognise feelings in others when you're familiar with feelings within yourself.

- Teaching yourself to pay attention to the emotional states within others.
- Improving your recognition of similarities between yourself and others. Your empathy for another person depends in part on seeing yourself as similar to that person.

Empathy is an important human trait. It helps us to understand our friends and neighbours, and even our enemies. It helps us to become more social.

Surely empathy is a trait worth cultivating.

Written by ; Richard Bayer

We could learn a lot from this notion of empathy when dealing with 'that person' who is always turning up pissed and we talk about him or her as though we have never seen or dealt with such a situation before. All we really need to do is look at ourselves and find our feelings and be honest with others. Try and put yourself in their shoes. Life is not a game where we can pretend that everything is alright. It's about those real issues that we wake up at night and sweat about. It may take years for you to realise that life has caught up with your ways, and it is better to stop the pretence now.

If you are interested, please carry on reading if not, I'm sure an off licence is open.

GARY WESTWELL OCTOBER 2005

ALCOHOLISM

Drinking alcohol socially and even beyond normal limits is now a regular part of everyday life. Some people go beyond normal drinking for some reason and if they are doing it day in and day out this can lead them onto the path of alcoholism. Or in my case, The Road To Alcoholism. Alcoholism is a disease, although many books separate alcoholism into two separate categories: alcohol abuse and alcohol dependence. Alcohol dependence is usually diagnosed using a questionnaire to help detect alcohol abuse.

If heavy alcohol dependency continues over a long period, the results can be serious with the classic diseases being contracted such as cirrhosis of the liver, pancreatitis, heart disease, hypertension and more. The majority of people prefer or are at least ignorant to the fact that they could seek help from a variety of people from different disciplines. Sadly, most people again, just don't bother and continue to see alcohol as just a 'happy juice' with a few unfortunate side effects. This can go on until it is just too late and they end up as just another statistic in the mortuary. Whilst admittedly alcoholism is not an easy nut to crack and in short you do not have to die of it. Treating alcoholism when it is very serious usually involves the person going through a period of detox which is then followed by counselling or attending a support group. While battling with drinking is usually a long road with a lot of pot holes, it can be achieved and you can get on with living a normal life.

FOREWORD

This book aims to describe how an apparently mentally 'normal' person in reasonable physical health and with no monetary or other obviously 'showing' worries spent a number years suffering with the effects of alcoholism and later managed to eventually regain a level of normality, and now prefers to describe himself as a non-drinking alcoholic. The effects of alcohol resulted in divorce, loss of employment, loss of a lot of money and a great deal of physical and mental illness. The story will not be uncommon to a number of people but may add as a reminder to them.

For others it may help them to keep away from the road I have described or prevent them from travelling further along it. The author describes real events which took place in the West Yorkshire Town of Huddersfield in the early 1970s until the present day. Hopefully, this work can provide a small insight into what is a very complex problem on which many professionals, the general public, and people with alcohol problems themselves have their own theories of 'what started it off' and what may 'cure it'. Often it describes situations which we can identify with personally or we have a close relative or friend who appears to be a 'carbon copy' of that person depicted in the story. Real names have been omitted for obvious reasons, but all other information is true to my knowledge, even though I admit that sadly due to the drink I cannot rely on perfect recall!

This book is the omnibus edition comprising the well received book 'THE ROAD TO BECOMING AN ALCOHOLIC AND THE WAY BACK' and 'ACOLHOLISM AND BEYOND' which is basically the book revisited with many more subjects and issues covered.

Hopefully, it may begin to answer some of the many questions regarding alcoholism that we often don't have time to ask or dare not ask while we are in certain situations like the doctors, or in a clinic or just on the telephone. I'm sorry that it is twice as long as the original book. I realised that trying to cover more of the questions and issues that have arisen over the past few months warranted a bigger book. It is also in larger print than usual mainly due to a popular request for something as easy to read as possible!

THE ROAD TO BECOMING AN ALCOHOLIC AND THE WAY BACK

LOOKING AT THE SIGNS

For many people, the facts about alcoholism are not very clear. For example, what is the difference between alcoholism and alcohol abuse? When should you seek help for a problem related to drinking?

For most people who drink, alcohol is a pleasant addition to our normal social activities. For example, I have never seen a man or a woman get ready to go out at night and feel happy to drink tea or coffee from a flask whilst they apply their make up and listen to their favourite C.D. We all need kicks in life, and alcohol is a cheap and relatively sure fire way of getting that kick in a controlled and legal way. Up to two drinks per day for men and one drink per day for woman is not harmful for most adults. In reality, these apparently normal limits are abused by practically everyone I ever meet. Most people survive totally unscathed by drinking and only a relative few hit the dizzy levels of alcoholism that I have done.

A standard drink is one 12 ounce bottle of beer, or one 5 ounce glass of wine, or 1.5 ounces of 80 % proof distilled spirits. However, a large number of people get into serious trouble because of their drinking habits. They either become an alcoholic and are dependent on alcohol or become an alcohol abuser.

The consequences of alcohol misuse are serious and in many situations, can be life threatening. It can increase the risk of certain cancers, especially those of the liver, oesophagus and the larynx (voice box). Heavy drinking can also cause liver cirrhosis, immune system damage and harm to the foetus during pregnancy. In addition, drinking increases the risks from car crashes as well as on the job injuries. Furthermore, homicides and suicides are more likely to be committed by persons who have been drinking. In purely economic terms, alcohol related problems cost society millions, however in human terms, the costs cannot be calculated.

Alcoholism, also known as 'alcohol dependence', is a disease that incorporates four main symptoms;

- Craving : A strong need, or compulsion, to drink.
- Loss of control : The inability to limit your drinking on any given occasion.
- Physical dependence : Withdrawal symptoms, such as nausea, sweating, shaking and anxiety occur when alcohol is stopped after a period of heavy drinking.
- Tolerance : The need to drink greater amounts of alcohol to 'get high.'

People who are not alcoholic sometimes do not understand why an alcoholic can have little willpower to stop drinking.

However, alcoholism has little to do with willpower when people are in the grip of a powerful 'craving' or uncontrollable need for alcohol that overrides the ability to stop drinking. This need can be as strong as the need for food or water.

Although some people are able to recover from alcoholism without help, the majority need assistance. With treatment and support, many people are able to stop drinking and rebuild their lives.

Many people wonder why some individuals can use alcohol without problems and others like myself crawl up and die at just the thought of a drink, why is this? and is their something in my past that could show me why I ended up as I did?

This part of the chapter now looks at what I feel were the early indicators of my alcoholism. Using my road analogy, as in the book title, I see it as 'looking at the signs' at the beginning of the journey. One important indicator could be linked to genetics. Scientists have found that having an alcoholic as a member of your family, makes it more likely that if you choose to also drink, you too may develop alcoholic tendencies.

I was born in 1960 in Blackburn, Lancashire. My parents were average middle class parents, my dad being an accountant by trade and my mother a shop worker. I have an older sister and an older brother, both appear to be happily married with two children each. There is no signs of excessive drinking from any of my family network or any problem areas which might be seen as a trigger to future drinking. As far as I can see, I had a normal happy childhood which continued through my schooldays and into early adulthood. This, to some extent, appears to bugger up my chances of proving it was all my mum and dad 's fault for genetically providing such a failure.

Could I now blame them for every time I made such a prat of myself at complete stranger's parties, in prison cells, off licences, in fact everywhere when I had had a drink? The answer to this question was obviously no! I had clearly not considered the complete story. In fact, scientists now believe that certain factors in the environment influence whether a person with a genetic risk for alcoholism ever develops the disease. A person's risk for developing alcoholism can increase based on the person's environment, including where and how he and she live, family, and culture and as I now know, how easy it is to get alcohol.

Following school and college, I joined a rock group and spent time touring and making records. My level of drinking up until this time was what

I would call average and did not show a concern to either myself or to others around me. I suppose I was the typical young drinker who could take it or leave it. Although I did thoroughly enjoy drinking at the appropriate 'official social events'. At the age of twenty one, I got my first 'proper job' as my mum would describe it. It was the choice between an interview with Timpson's selling shoes or at (would you believe) Storthes Hall Psychiatric Hospital as a trainee nurse. I must admit it was not really choice at all, as I did not have the necessary one O'Level in maths which was required in order to sell shoes. I moved on to qualify as a psychiatric nurse and later as a social worker.

At the time, I was earning a good wage and living in a nice house and had plenty of what I would call, 'understandable work pressures.'

My biggest regret at the time was not ending my poor marriage. Work seemed to become more difficult to endure and I began to take solace in the bottle. The changes in my drinking patterns were numerous. Firstly, rather than enjoying a drink in the evening with friends in the pub, the drink became the key issue and it took place mainly at home and often alone, in private. Secondly, the amount of alcohol consumed steadily increased. Lastly, and worst of all, secret conversations about the amount I was drinking became a 'normal ' activity. I began to confirm my earlier fears that I had when working as a psychiatric nurse, but like happens when you are a 'professional' I did not think that it related to me. I was becoming a person who abused alcohol.

Alcohol abuse differs from alcoholism in that it does not include an extremely strong addiction to alcohol, loss of control over drinking, or physical dependence. Alcohol abuse is defined as a pattern of drinking that results in one or more of the following situations in a 12 month period :

- Failure to fulfil major work, school, or home responsibilities.
- Drinking in situations that are physically dangerous, such as while driving a car or operating machinery;
- Having recurring alcohol related legal problems, such as being arrested by the police under the influence of alcohol or by physically

hurting someone while drunk; and

- Continued drinking despite having ongoing relationship problems that are caused or worsened by the drinking.

Although alcohol abuse is technically different from alcoholism, personally I feel I have a mixture of both, which I know I will always battle with to a certain extent.

Perhaps a big step forward in tackling the alcoholism and the alcohol abuse is recognising the signs of the problem. How can you tell whether you may have a drinking problem? The four following questions are often very difficult for the average person to answer, without running the risk of them being inadvertently found 'out', but they nearly always make the person blush at best and at worst try their up most to tell you that it is me that has the problem, so why am I asking them about it?

Try asking yourself or a close friend if you dare :

- Have you ever felt you should cut down on your drinking?

- Have people annoyed you by criticizing your drinking?

- Have you ever felt bad about your drinking?

- Have you ever had a drink first thing in the morning (as an eye opener) to steady the nerves or to get rid of a hangover?

One 'yes' answer suggests a possible alcohol problem. If you answered 'yes' to more than one question, it is highly likely that a problem exists. This may seem depressingly familiar to some of you as it certainly does to me and if so, you may wish to read on and even more importantly go and see your G.P.

Even if you answered 'no' to all of the above questions, if you come across drink related problems with your job, relationships, health or the police you should look for help. Again, your G.P. is a good place to start. The effects of alcohol can be extremely serious and even fatal, both to you and to others.

A BIT OF HISTORY

As a preamble to the main text, I felt it was interesting to look at some of the past professionals of the art of drinking too much, and remind myself that at least with beer, things have remained the same for hundreds of years. Drink has always existed and so have drunks. Blackburn where I was born was no different to anywhere else, except for that bloody great big brewery Twaites's looking over the rest of the town.

Around 1920 in Blackburn, local character Tommy Allan, a builder's labourer, was on board one of Nuttal's Brewery Drays. The dray had a car precariously perched on the back advertising the beer. After a day out advertising the beer, they had sampled just a bit too much themselves

He and the dray driver arrived back at the brewery and they were both said to be 'in their cups' (drunk) and tried to drive a car off the back of the dray. It's funny how things never seem to change after getting yourself drunk, and entering the new world of semi madness. We've all done it and many of us will continue to do it unless like me you find that it is too damaging to your physical and mental health and daren't touch the stuff.

BLACKBURN

I lived in Blackburn in the early 1960's before I moved to the sunny, humorous and free loving Huddersfield. O.K. so I made it up about it being sunny all the time, and humorous and free loving. I'm not really sure what the fascination was for satanic mills and the toil of all working in the cotton mills for all the hours that God would send just to live in houses like those. The one smell I did tend to like even from a very young age was the smell of hops which came from Thwaites brewery.

I also love the sixties even to this day. I remember........Sitting on the pavement curb at the front of our house in Palmer Street. My short M&S pants showing my very thin and hairless legs supported by a pair of Startright brown sandals and grey school socks. The tar in between the cobbles was red hot in Summer and I couldn't resist poking at it with a stick. 'I love Jennifer Eccles, I know that she loves me....la la la la la la la.....' drinking fizzy pop and Smiths Crisps sat outside a pub with my brother and sister in our Wolsley 1600 in 1967.

The world was a brighter, more cheerful place in those days......going the 25 miles to Blackpool, fish n' chips on the way back listening to the Adams singers....'Sing something simple'.

Jimmy Clitheroe, Sandy Powel, Charlie Drake and Billy Smarts Circus, ah I remember those days. I also remember a boy who I found fascinating, kissing a girl in Corporation Park, I think that was all they were doing. Things were wonderful on that hot summers day, until he told me to fuck off then carried on with his necking. I did 'Fuck off' and ran home to ask my mum what it meant. A clip round the ear as far as I was concerned. This was one of my first tastes of the real world that I can remember, and I realised that life was not always going to be a bed of roses. I liked Blackburn, however, looking at past pictures, I think my dad made the right decision to move to 'uddersfield' in 1969.

Like many young lads in the mid 1960's, I loved to watch things being knocked down. In Blackburn this was a perfected art form as row after row of terraced houses was destroyed day after day. Houses were flattened in the name of progress, two years before I left Blackburn to live in my spanking new home in Huddersfield. This is where I have lived ever since, trying to perfect my Yorkshire accent which used to return to a Lancashire twang whenever I had too much to drink without me even realising. Anyway, lets go back to the subject of drinking, which I'm sure the people reading this book will be more interested in than a load of terraced houses being demolished, although I must admit, I wasn't at the time.

MOOD SWINGS

As the 'normal Gary Westwell' I have always been regarded by others as a 'thinker'. On the face of it, this could mean I'm a bright intelligent man who likes to analyse the world, work out the pitfalls, and generally put the world to right. Unfortunately, none of these notions are true, it would be wonderfully romantic if they were true and I could sit contemplating my navel and write poetry as a living. The reality is I'm not a deep intelligent thinker but I do think a lot.

The problem with my type of thinking is the tendency to ruminate for hours on end about the most piddling of subjects, which most people would disregard almost immediately. I have always been melodramatic and from being a young child I would 'run away' from home at the slightest of excuses or run home from school which was only about two hundred yards away! Life was so hard for me in those days, what with having to tie my own shoe laces when my big sister wasn't instantly on call and many other such traumatic events.

As I got older, I don't think my mind

and attitude changed very much at all, I continued to muse over things and would blow things out of all proportion. I also realised that I thrived off adulation and was never happier than when I was the centre of attention. Although I did not particularly like playing the drums, I did love the attention it brought me, and when I first saw my picture in the newspapers that was it, I was addicted to attention, however big or small. In retrospect, I would have been just as happy playing the mouth organ, as long as I was at the front and people could see me. Being in hospital surrounded by medical staff also produced the same effect of attention seeking as I acted out my part of being an ill man but it some how didn't give me the same buzz as signing autographs!

I always strived for being the best at what I was doing at the time, this didn't matter whether I was in an egg and spoon race or wheel barrow race with my dad holding on for dear life, exam results or playing the drums in my bands, I was only happy if we won or were successful. In short, I was a pain in the arse I suppose for the people who had to endure me. Don't get me wrong, I was a popular lad but only if things went my way in life. As I have now matured to the age of forty five I have still not cracked this part of my life but I am at least aware that I am a pain in the arse!

My biggest problem, is not that of the attention seeking, which most people tended to be able to cope with, but the drastic mood swings which result from alcohol consumption.

One thing which became very scary to both myself and to the other people around me was the shear speed of the swing in mood, from pure elation and downright silliness where I loved everybody, to a feeling of absolute misery without anybody actually saying anything. I could walk along my village centre and in the time it took me to smoke a cigarette I was back on a downer again and would go and hide in the graveyard reading all the grave stones and then looking next door at the writings in the grounds of the non - drinking Methodist Chapel. Over time I spent time at the G.P.s and various other medical experts trying to cure my so called depression with tablets, non of which did the blindest bit of good. I realised this was not depression in it's true sense and the mood swings and general bad temperedness were almost certainly all attributable to the amount of alcohol I was drinking. How was I able to change from a shy unassuming person to an absolute monster within minutes? Well, it sadly wasn't rocket science it was dependent on how much I could drink in the shortest time possible and then hold on to it until I found enough money to buy some more. I found my self arguing about anything whether it made sense or not, music, money, why every body else was wrong?, the list goes on. Unfortunately I have a long protracted history of having a big gob and the alcohol just made this worse. If you could have been fined for consistently insulting people I would have been broke many years ago. I am also an extremely vain person who looks in mirrors at the slightest of opportunities and insults regarding how other people look came as second nature. If I saw someone who was thinning on top or who had rotten teeth I would pounce on these facts, when I was drunk I would get steadily worse and would be totally unaware of what I was doing or saying. Once sober I could only cringe at my actions, that's if I could remember them.

TRYING TO SURVIVE

For me, drink, as many people will have experienced, changes the way of looking at every day issues. We all know the saying 'I've never been to bed with an ugly woman, but I sure as hell have woke up with a few'. This saying, although trashy in content and hopefully not true for the majority of us, thankfully!, does have a better meaning when placed in a wider context. There is no doubt about it, we have all felt more confident after a drink, more assertive and able to handle almost anything for a short while. We have also felt the after effects of alcohol. That feeling of acute embarrassment at something we have said or done in front of our friends or even worse the feeling of timid ness, vulnerability and wanting to stay in bed until mid afternoon just in case you may meet up with the person you were so confident with the night before. With a really bad ' hang over' these feelings can become so bad that if you don't have a few pints at dinner time to top you up you cannot function properly and have a lower confidence level than before your first drink the night before.

In my experience very few people are prepared to talk about alcohol. If they do, it is said within certain strict limitations. In the scenario mentioned above it is often talked about over a few pints the night after and restricted to finding out whether they really did 'show themselves up' and comments such as 'I don't think I had that much more than everybody else do you?'. After this, people often console themselves by finding someone else who behaved far worse than they did and then the shutters come down on the conversation. Life moves on until the next time. Someone else now has the problem.

In reality, they DID show themselves up and the conversation about how pissed they had really been is conducted elsewhere out of earshot and therefore knowledge of the concerned individual. This pattern of behaviour is not uncommon amongst normal drinkers who happen to have just gone on a session at the office party or on a hen night with others who end up in virtually the same state. This pattern often begins to change however when a number of other ingredients enter the scene.

What if the bender begins to get longer? and you

cannot feel comfortable going out without a small snifter just to get the cogs in motion. what if you have more than just a hard job to do and it is compounded by a relationship problem ? Many of us have been in these situations and have survived the ordeal of it leading into alcoholism but what of those who haven't survived like myself? What magical thing has happened which gives me the deserved title of alcoholic?

THE SLIPPERY SLOPE

For a while I loved it! The alcohol could certainly make me feel good. Learning to drink in a morning was a revelation to me. At first, hangovers did not last very long and after a few gulps of Special Brew I was back alive, and rarely felt sick. I would have the cans in the morning (usually two) whilst I was still in my solitary bed. It was exciting to think that in a few_minutes I would change from a depressed and quite man into a person who was capable of anything. Once I had had a wee I would clamber back into the haven of a bed and drift away into my own world. I would still wake without any alarm clock and as I didn't have to drive to work any more since to save money we had decided months earlier that we could manage with one car, I could relax. Amazingly, my wife never accused me of drinking before work and it is still a myth to me how she very rarely seemed to smell it in the car. At work I was now mainly office based and would scrounge lifts where necessary. Inevitably, over time I began to drink whilst I was at work by taking longer and longer dinner times. I also gained the taste, advantages and speed of drinking vodka whilst in a rush. Towards beer which was much slower to get and keep down without puking, vodka was a god send. In addition, I had been told that it was not as easy to smell on the breath and therefore I felt much more at ease when entering a meeting. Again, to my surprise I was never challenged at work regarding the subject. As I maintained earlier in the book, people do not often talk about someone who is drinking a lot to their face and prefer to talk to others about their friend's problem. This means the person will only usually be confronted when it is too late and often get sacked for some other reason.

Following a dismal days work where I would sometimes be firing on very few if any cylinders, I would try and make my way back home. I did sometimes get a lift back home but preferred to go on the bus or walk which gave me the excuse to down a few legitimately and more slowly in a pub. Its funny how you begin to enjoy and then rely on your own company in the pub thinking that the less people who see you there the better. Before I got home, I would ensure I had enough cans to set me off again in the morning , carrying a non descript bag to hide my gains. It must have seemed funny if not hilarious to witness the suited gentleman from up the road calmly walking towards his garden wall to find his hiding place night after night. I left the house for good, having found a woman at work who drunk very little and was prepared to drive me around and was at first, unaware of the amount I was drinking. This did not last long, and following a honeymoon period of sleeping in her car, going to the pub and not doing very much else to be honest, I went to live with her in a

dilapidated old cottage which was infested with mice. The property was rented and due to my drinking and lack of enthusiasm for anything, nothing was done to improve our living environment. I began to drink more and more both in the house and in the pub. The drink became a way of life and was constantly in my thoughts. I was by this time, beginning to realise but would not admit it to myself, that drink was controlling me and not me the drink. My perception of reality was also altering big time. I felt the house was a beautiful, idyllic cottage. I did not see the mice, the clutter or the dirt. The house was fine and merely needed a few D.I.Y. repairs carrying out and I was the man to do it, just give me a bit more time………The jobs, of course were never done and I continued to deteriorate both physically and mentally. One morning I woke very early, probably about five, and disappeared downstairs for my fix. At the time, I was drinking about thirteen cans a day at home and more when out, I was also technically working. In addition, I was lasting around two hours at any time of day or night before I physically needed another drink. After firstly being sick in a box in the cellar (which was now my regular morning routine) I then blatantly found a can of cheap, strong cider which was the only thing I could afford in bulk by this time, and hurriedly attempted to sup it down. Instead of feeling my usual bum's rush I immediately puked the lot. I was not too concerned and put it down to the quality of the cider and opened a can of Special Brew instead. I was like a dream, you know, the one where earlier, the plane you were able to fly quite easily and competently to evade the enemy, but now as hard as you try to start it, will not get off the ground. I attempted to drink but would immediately return it to the floor. I panicked and realised that the game was being played to different rules now. The room span and ducked and dived uncontrollably, so I returned to bed with the can firmly clutched in my hand. The bed also began to spin as I held on to the back of it for dear life. This was not how I had imagined it, George Best had just fallen in the gutter, felt a bit pissed, then woken up with a beautiful woman and a wedge of money scattered over the bed hadn't he? Now I was not sure, but I was sure that I needed help and fast.

HOSPITAL

The ambulance appeared surreal. I had been moved by stretcher into the back of the van by a man who I knew from my past as being a student nurse, and he was now a paramedic. I didn't have the will nor the energy to go through the general niceties of asking how he was doing in his career that was pretty obvious, better than me! This was the real world of knowing you are at real risk of dying and I was scared. The oxygen mask was put on and my blood pressure taken. The real scary thing was, not that the ambulance people didn't know what they were doing, they did, but that everything appeared to be so normal and routine to them. It was, and I was just another punter who had balls himself up and was now paying the price. Gary, do you have any allergies?…..whose your next of kin? ……… Who cares? I drifted away at times and just wanted to stay alive, no more and no less.

Once in casualty, the questions were repeated by another nurse and a junior doctor and it all began to get on my nerves. Don't they realise who I am? I'm not your average patient who you deal with everyday? I'm Gary, John Westwell from Blackburn in Lancashire and I'm beginning to go dizzy again. I was later told by my partner that I had nearly fallen off the trolley on numerous occasions and had puked everywhere.

I woke, with a feeling of somebody pulling or pushing a large tube up and down my throat. In reality, I had suffered a fit induced by the alcohol and had been quickly moved to 'resuss' a word I had commonly known in my previous life as a nurse as being close to death. I was really up shit creek this time.

When I finally was placed on the ward, I fully began to take in the reality of the situation. I'd been found out! There was no going to work for me today, no dinner time session and no return from work for my nightly bender. All that engulfed my fragile mind, was what will people think? and what will they say at work? It's funny how one minute your close to death and the next your preoccupied with thinking such futile, inappropriate, trivialities. I was back home in a few days, with neither alcohol or its associated problems rarely mentioned again by the doctors or nursing staff, after all this was a general hospital who were interested in getting you better physically. 'Ponsey' things like dealing with people with drink problems were dealt with by psychiatrists and psychologists in other clinics, weren't they? I fully agreed of course, there was nothing much wrong with me. All I needed was a short spell at home to physically recover, to tell work my blood pressure had been high and Bob's your uncle! Oh..... it's good to be back to normality. Like many people in such situations I was just not ready to give up the life I had lead for ten years or so, not just yet anyway. It didn't matter that I had been close to death my mind wasn't able to cope with such things. All I wanted to do underneath it all at this stage in my life was to forget about it all and carry on as I had done with as little fuss as possible.

HOME AGAIN

Now sober, everything in the house looked and seemed different. It was a complete tip, there were half empty cans, clothes strewn every where, and puke patches left in every room. My, initial priority was to ring work and convince them that all was well. I rang, and talked to good old Peter the administrator who knew everyone and everything, he assured me that everything was fine and that everybody was concerned about my blood pressure and had told me to rest and not too come back too early. After all, remember, I was a middle manager with the social services department and an ex-nurse, such people are too experienced to suffer from alcoholism aren't they? I felt relieved and satisfied that all was well, I could relax with this notion.

Things were looking up, I was sober, the house was a tip but I had returned to work and my divorce money from my house sale was due. I shortly moved to a new house in a new village, which I bought myself, and carried on living with my partner. Then the rot set in again, I had lasted around five weeks without a drink but I knew

new deep down that I was not able to last forever. I felt I was able to just cut down and that I would not repeat the scenario I went through only weeks before. I had been found out by my partner, my mum, and my close friends and they were all aware of where I had been and that I should not repeat it again.

I began to slowly build up my old habits and was drinking Special Brew again. I was buying my cans from the only shop in the village and I was sure they more than suspected that I had a problem. The shopkeeper was very discreet and never flinched when I went in time and time again. I was also hiding beer again, and was once questioned in the local pub about why I used to search the litter bins after closing time nearly every night. The truth was, I was beginning to forget where I had left them! I thought I had solved this problem by hiding the cans closer to home so that no one would twig what I was doing.

I decided to hide my cans in my own wheelie bin and collect them at my leisure. There was always a major problem for me if I ran out drink and I needed to be secure that there was enough to keep me going. On one occasion however, my plans went disastrously wrong. One morning, when I was particularly frail and in need of a drink, I spent about ten minutes looking out of the living room windows to ensure that the coast was clear for my collection and morning session. I waved at passers by and greeted the postman, it was very usual for me to greet anyone. I must have been in a good mood, probably because I had spent the last of my money on a good stash of cans which were ready for just picking up and opening from the bins outside the front door. Unfortunately, I

saw the bin men arrive and confiscate my bin and the beer carefully hidden inside. It was time for another hiding place.

VICIOUS CIRCLE

The predictable cycle of heavy drinking, physical recovery, the 'it won't happen again syndrome', guilt and depression, followed by a gradual build up of drinking again, continued for the next two years or so. In this period, I experienced the typical effects this behaviour can have on a person. I lost my job, was barred from the local pub for fighting, got into trouble with the police and narrowly escaped a prison sentence, I spent a number of periods in general and psychiatric hospitals, moved house again, my partner left me for good and in short, I was in a complete mess. The more 'famous' I became as the 'family alcoholic' and local drunk, the worse I became. I thought of myself as a complete shit and felt that I had nothing to lose or gain.

I had the attitude of being able to handle my self both physically and academically when drinking and when talking to counsellors, doctors and my family and friends. Many people told me that I was killing my self. My doctor told me that I had probably around two years to live and that only 2% of alcoholics ever pull through. I listened, I gave the correct well trained academic responses and then quickly forgot. Inside, I was never fully convinced, It was as though they were talking about another person, and it was not really me they were referring to. It was that bloke who I always see in town who was always carrying a bag and asking me for the price of a cup of tea, which he managed to buy from the off licence whenever I obliged him. I watched all the documentaries on the telly and I managed to convince myself they were not like me. In truth, I knew the doctors, counsellors, and even the T.V. programmes were right and I could not kid my self any longer. Of course I did………..

I still had semi sober moments where I could half convince people for a short while that I was getting better, usually by telephone conversations so that no one could smell my breath and realise that I was still in my underpants and hadn't had a shave for a week. I used the telephone a lot and if I could have rung for my drink and have it delivered I would have done. My dog who couldn't answer back, became my best friend, until he pissed all over my bed and the laminate floor or he needed a long walk, which was becoming ever harder to do.

I had a few friends and relatives who would help me get by, and I am sure they had had enough of me, and often didn't know what to do for the best with me. Do I leave him to wallow in his own shit and puke and self pity?, do I bring him a few cans and hope he will gradually come off it or do I give him a strong bollocking and tell him the errors of his ways? I'm not sure whether any of these methods would have done any good at this particular time. My mum, who had always stuck by me was understandably, at the end of her tether.

I'm not sure to be honest, what particular event or happening actually occurred, that began my realisation that I had finally reached rock bottom. Was it the time I slept on top of a grave stone in the local church all night and thought that my mobile phone was an S.A.S. walki talki ? Was it the time I had a shit behind a skip in the middle of the village centre, and was only saved by the fact that it was only six in the morning and I was heading for one of the off licences which would usually serve me? Was it one of the times when even the off licences wouldn't have me because it was too early for even me or I had tried to sell the shopkeepers wife my watch for enough to buy another can. Unfortunately, I don't think it was any of these isolated events. I did not find Jesus, nor any other singular event which suddenly showed me the errors of my ways. In short, I was sick of it. I was sick of feeling sick and of thinking about it, something had to change. As well as hating the drink I began to hate anything connected with it. I would find my self stuck in the corner of a pub with no mates and no money tearing up beer mats. However, I still found that I had to reach towards the bar to get yet another drink. I would not leave a pub situation until I had got somebody mad enough to hit me or the bar man had intervened before this could happen. Often, I could not understand what the problem had been as I was thrown out of the door, having just pebbled dashed another toilet and broken the holder. Insulting other people became one of my biggest past times. The bigger the person the bigger the insult, and the bigger the bruise. More often than not I would deserve the verbal and physical bollocking I would receive but on other occasions it was not on. I would sometimes be picked on by a puny little no hoper who had found his place to shine in the pub containing three people and me. How I longed by this time, to see some sort of guiding light to break my world of disasters. It was going to be some time before this was going to happen.

On a Friday night, I still would attempt to find my way into town after spending hours limbering up at home. This was not vanity, I was not limbering up mentally to go out, I had already drunk plenty enough to go out by mid afternoon in my mind. It was physically that the problems were challenging. I would go out with a friend I had known for years and had trained as a social worker with. He was fully aware that I was an alcoholic and no type of pretence was necessary. He was also a stable drinker who could take it or leave it and often took his car when we went out.

THE BLIPS

What can I say about blips? What the hell are they anyway? The first time I heard this expression was when I was at my mum's house and I thought she was just trying to be kind. I had remained off alcohol for some time but I had relented back to my old ways, which you may say is entirely typical of a long standing alcoholic, and deserves all the clichéd statements which people of all kinds say or shout at you. 'After all we've done and you let us down' I learned to accept this and although I certainly didn't ignore it or use it as an excuse to carry on drinking, I did try and put it into perspective. I needed not to dwell on this blip and concentrate on rectifying the drink pattern as soon as possible. The prognosis was reasonably good, firstly I had not intended to get myself blathered, secondly I wish I hadn't done very soon afterwards and thirdly I wanted to immediately come off it again.

None of us are perfect, and stopping drinking altogether is never going to be easy, and for most of today's normal population it would be downright impossible. As you can see this is a very short bit about the subject of blips, and as many alcoholics will tell you, the shorter time spent on them the better for all concerned.

BREAKING THE PATTERN

As I got ready on a Friday night, I would sometimes drink too much even to my standards and fall asleep having half buttoned a shirt and left the tap running ready for a shave in the bath room. I would wake just in time to prevent another flood.

Living alone wasn't easy, but getting used to it was worse. I developed my own ways of doing things and this included which songs I would listen to in the house and the jobs I would do and those I would choose not to do. After all it was my house and I didn't have many pleasures left. I would rekindle bands I had listened to for ages in the past like the Small Faces and The Who and act out a complete stage set in front of the dog. Eventually, even the dog had had enough and it was time for me to go out. On one occasion, I went to a night club and met my present partner. At first, I thought I would last about the length of a dance and that would be it. A few drinks later and I was still hanging on in there, I was interested. My partner did not dwell initially on how much I was still drinking but began to pick up on my mum's attitude to the heavy drinking. The trick was to concentrate on the times I was not drinking rather than on those times when I was. I was still in and out of hospital with a mixture of basic physical detox initially, followed by a few group counselling sessions if the staff had time. As one clearly disillusioned member of staff told me, 'this is just like very expensive bed and board with a bit of therapy thrown in' I did not argue. The staff did not show empathy for any of the predicaments which I confessed to and insisted on relying on a medical model of nursing by taking my T.P.R. and B.P. at every opportunity. It took me many months and in fact a year or so before I realised that repeatedly going back to hospital was not the solution. The answer to the drink problem was much more complicated but at the same time very basic, relying on simple rules and ideas. The first task, was to not break the pattern of drinking but to slow it down. I had now drunk to varying degrees ever since I was fifteen and had had a problem with it for about five years. It was now physically and even more so mentally impossible for me to stop drinking overnight. What I needed to do was to give myself permission to drink if necessary at first, and rely on the fact that I now did not want to really drink and that over time I would get sufficiently sick of it. In short, what was really happening was the fact that no one was telling me to stop drinking I was telling myself and doing something about it. This method of detox is not the quick fix option and will not work on a person who feels he or she is only stopping drinking for others. You must see the reason to stop drinking as fundamentally for yourself and then recognise that other people may benefit from your actions but this is not your prime objective. I would love to sit down and write beautiful grammatical prose about the new world in which I was now living thanks to the therapeutic intervention of a Swedish eminent doctor. It appears selfish at first I must admit, but I feel if is the only true answer. You need to rid yourselves of the need to begin to feel honest and good to your best mate or partner and concentrate on making sure that you really are lowering the amount of drink you were consuming. Initially, it does not really matter whether the people close to you know you are trying to get onto the wagon as long as you know. After all, you have proved for years how good you are at hurriedly drinking a pint of larger at the bar and then carrying your legitimate drink and your partner's back to your table. Everyone else is deceived by your antics and they don't really give a toss any way. You must have the attitude of being sick of alcohol and wanting to really stop the habit. Therefore, firstly you must realise that <u>you</u> have a problem with drinking, and are fed up with it. Secondly, realise that others also think that you have a problem but do not dwell on what they think. It is of little use arguing who has got the problem and also just deciding you both have it, but their problem is slightly worse than yours. You have the problem, and it is you who you need to concentrate on to overcome it. Regarding everyone else, let them drink what they like and come to their own conclusions as to whether they need to slow down a bit, it is not your problem. Do not concentrate on how much you are drinking, look at why you need to drink so much. If you have got as far as this in the book you are interested in alcohol for some reason and are probably a drinker yourself. The key issue, is to concentrate on yourself and not what others think.

Other people will soon pick up on the fact that you are more reliable and begin to speak a lot more sense. As you begin to drink less your memory capacity will increase although some of the things you have done will be lost forever, thank god. Your diet, bowel movements and appetite will all improve as long as you cut steadily down. Of course, you will have blips and sometimes total failures where you feel as though you are back at square one again. This will affect you most where others continue to treat you as though you have just had a skin full, and really you are having a much lower amount and on far fewer occasions than you used to. Remember, it does not matter what other people think, particularly regarding your potential to succeed in getting to grips with alcohol. For me, I had to know that eventually I would become so tired of drinking that there was no reason to continue for others, they will always need a drink and manage by keeping it within reasonable limits. Unfortunately, this decision is yours and yours alone, ultimately. However, other people can either help or hinder the process.

FRIENDS, RELATIVES
and THE PROFESESSIONALS

Although I have clearly said that it must be you who makes the decisions as to when, how and what is drunk and how you are going to lead your future life, you will continue to be influenced by others as you always have been. Regarding alcohol, the influence others have on your behaviour must be kept to a minimum, you must be the person in control. You should drink at your pace and drink what you decide to drink, or be like me don't drink at all if this is what suits you. To stop the persuasion of someone don't put your self in the position to be able to choose different options. Don't stand in a pub pondering over whether you should have a half or a pint, don't go to the pub in the first place, then you don't have a choice to make as to whether you have a drink or not. Obviously drinking is much harder in the first few weeks when the physical symptoms of withdrawal are at their greatest. It is during this time that I personally needed mentally and physically restraining from taking another drink. My partner was able to help me by watering down the alcohol in reducing dosages at first until I had overcome this phase. After a few days I was able to tell her that I was aware that she had watered down the drink but it still kept me going.

Its funny now to think of how different people react to a situation where you are under the influence and they are not, or when you have in their eyes, crossed the line and been in hospital due to drinking. I found that close friends and relatives would speak to you using a third person or shout at you if they were in fear of not being understood. Does he want another cigarette instead of a drink ? my mum would say, I'm standing next to you mum, on your left I would reply, I KNOW my mum would say. Oh ?....... I tried to keep such conversations to a minimum. My mum was also able to forget that I was a trained nurse and a social worker and I would be reduced to an adolescent who needed all his thinking and decisions made for him. In retrospect this was probably true but was certainly annoying at the time. The 'professionals' I encountered were sometimes even funnier than my mum and certainly at times of less use. The psychiatrist I encountered on the whole was a reasonably jovial

Indian man, who oozed pride at his own success and would unknowingly repeat tales which he felt were helpful and had relevance and street cred to me. He told me on at least three occasions what <u>his</u> most important priorities in life were and how to go about achieving them. Although he was married and had children they were not mentioned in his list of priorities for life. Instead, they included his car as his top priority, followed by his house and then the fact that he was a Doctor and wanted to remain as such and keep his name on the register. I suspect this last point was aimed specifically at the fact that I had spent so much time in hospital that he felt that others would accuse him of keeping me there just for the money. As if. Just after my last stay at a private hospital it closed down the psychiatric wing but failed to replace it with any other services. This is probably another reason why I no longer drink, the choice of entering a hospital for those first few day of detox have gone. I feel that although it is in a sense a good thing to remove the hospital 'tag' to alcohol recovery and to keep people in their own homes, it is a risky business which could go drastically wrong. This is shown, earlier on in the book where I was fitting due to alcohol withdrawal and nearly bit my own tongue off.

G.P.s have a similar effect on me. Alcohol appears to be a big issue for them to handle, and most try to limit its attention to the ten minute slot which is designated to everybody else at the surgery, regardless of the level of need at the time. The ten minutes has consisted of two entirely different approaches. Firstly, there has been the look of, …. 'I know you look ill and look like you desperately need something to calm you down but I just don't know whether you are committed enough'. Should I just be dead, and show real commitment to giving up? Then there are the more realistic types who know they are going to hand over the medication in the end and decide that delaying the process will only increase my chances of doing a runner or puking all over the surgery carpet.

In a nut a shell, the G.P.s I have seen have been O.K. but with their own admittance they cannot solve your problem. They can stop you feeling sick and make you feel as though you are wasting their valuable and very limited time but in the whole scheme of things they are a very small cog in a very big wheel and the sooner people realise this the better. You are the main part of that big wheel and although we all spend a long time blaming everyone and everything else for our drinking habits, it is us who take the ultimate responsibility for our destiny.

MY CHILDREN, PARTNER AND ALCOHOL

The following is a short excerpt from a small scrapbook which my daughter produced one frenzied afternoon to desperately try and help me to stop drinking. After much thought and deliberation as to whether it was a good idea to give me the book, she was persuaded to do so by my partner. She cautiously presented it to me shortly after I had been discharged from hospital after yet another bout of heavy drinking followed no doubt by arguments and an ambulance having to be called as I fell into a lump of shit on the settee, or floor or maybe I was caught earlier downing yet another pint or two in the garden? Who knows my memory does not work that well at times, perhaps its because I didn't want it to do? My daughter gave me the book with the full encouragement of both my partner and my slightly older son. Typically, as with most things and was usual at the time with anything which might evoke emotions and the risk of upset due to the reality of the situation, the message did not fully register and after a tertiary glance, it was left on the shelf with other pieces of advice and small notes which I had accumulated without really noticing.

My daughter was nine years old at the time of writing this short but succinct note:

THINK BEFORE YOU DRINK

TO DAD,

I HAVE MADE THIS SCRAPBOOK FOR YOU, SO WHEN YOU FEEL LIKE YOU WANT A DRINK YOU CAN LOOK THROUGH IT, AND IT WILL HOPEFULLY HELP YOU NOT TO DRINK. SO PLEASE READ THIS, WHEN YOU FEEL LIKE THIS BECAUSE IT IS SO IMPORTANT THAT YOU DON'T EVER DRINK BECAUSE YOU END UP DRUNK AND HURTING YOUR FAMILY.

LOTS OF LOVE   XXX

There's not much I feel that I could add to the above message in terms of both common good sense and pure heartfelt emotion that these simple words began to describe to me once I sobered up and I got a grip of my self.

Life wasn't about me giving the kids material presents or just saying I sorry, no it was about me keeping off the alcohol and being fit enough both mentally and physically, to show that I loved them and was interested in them. It was about time that I took control of my self and stopped, pardon the expression, disappearing up my own arsehole every time some thing (or quite truthfully nothing!) went slightly pear shaped and I turned to the bottle and did not give my kids, family and friends a second thought but wallowed I self pity. Whilst I'm on a role at this point, I feel I must also acknowledge and appreciate the worry, despair, pain and the anguish that I put both my mother and my partner through as they had to witness first hand the moaning, strange, aggressive and to put it bluntly, the bloody awful person I had turned into. The sad thing is, they had little if any choice in the matter! I decided to drink and short of them disowning me altogether they had to pick up the pieces and pretended that all was well to other people. My partner had to continue to work and my mum had to face the dreaded bus to town in a morning when I'm sure people had seen me flat on my face only hours earlier.

I have often have been 'sent to my mums' and banished from my house when I became too much for my partner to stand and lived at my mums until I was fit enough to return home. My mum who can be likened to living with a racehorse commentator who is addicted to speed and she is telling me off at full throttle has put up with a lot at the best of times, and particularly when I have been coming down from alcohol and virtually climbing the walls. Personally I wouldn't have given me the time of day, never mind almost wipe my arse in these times of alcoholism. In short, if you were to meet me in these times of indulgence, any body who was not obsessed by sado masochism would run a mile and plead to never have to return. In time, these close family members, if your lucky, will return if you can change your behaviour. This means changing the ways you both think and act when confronted with drink in every situation in your future life, and not just those first few days you return from detox. Whether you like it or not people whether they are initially your best mate, your lover, or your mum, they will always begin any abstinence regime you can think of however severe, like locking your self in a cage or moving to a desert island with a certain distrust that you will be drinking again soon. This is entirely understandable as many of us do. You may moan about this and not fully understand why they continue to openly search for the missing cans and bottles for months to come and people do not whole heartedly invite you to their houses sometimes for years but this is reality, would you if it was the other way round and they had made your life a misery for years. There is no easy way of getting round this problem or speeding this part of recovery up.

THE FUTURE

Right, so the drinking appears to be sorted and under control. I feel physically and mentally healthy and life is looking and feeling good considering my position in the past. But what about the future?, will I just last out for a short while and then bang! Just imagine I see a mate in the middle of town who is unaware of what a mess I have been in the past and he buys me a drink in one of the old haunts, just for old times sake? Or, disaster strikes and my partner packs me in and I've nothing to do but to walk to the most hidden and cheapest corner shop and down my sorrows? The answer to these dilemmas will never be an easy one and I know that I will probably have to fight the addiction for evermore. It is not the first sniff of alcohol, or even the first small drink which would grip me into submission leaving me wide open to have a skinful. No sadly, it is often that hint of a hangover for the first time which looms. Most people can overcome hangovers like a drunk can overcome severe bruising after a fall, but like I pointed out early in this book once the addictive nature of the illness kicks in your snookered for a while.

The good news is that as time continues to pass and people begin to respect you for not drinking or at least don't automatically cross over the street and instead begin to speak to you in a mature and adult manner, you feel that you do not want to let the side down or let yourself down. I'm not talking about the ability to withstand another onslaught of puking and shitting yourself before you have had time to remove your trousers, no the problem is much more serious if you allow it to take a grip of you.

The test will always relate to the unknown fact that at any time I may have to deal with a major disaster in my life. Unfortunately, you do not have the chance to practice what you would do in the event of the death of a loved one or a major real illness which you are suddenly told about and I have learned to think of other strategies to deal with such things. On a less morbid note, I have found that there are many things you can do and actually enjoy that doesn't involve drinking or going to the local on a regular basis. At present, I am attempting to complete a law degree and I am back playing with my rock band with the same group of people I last played with in 1978, although this time without any alcohol in sight! With the degree I do not aspire to earn mega bucks as a result, my aim is to remain sober and healthy, and if it helps to add structure to my life to a certain extent and helps me to think about life from the other side of the coin that will do for me. Although, a gig at the little building below wouldn't go a miss!

We have also bought a dog again which although
It brings back memories of my old dog called Max
(just in case you were interested) in terms of being
a pain in the arse at times, particularly when it
needs cleaning up, it can be a great therapy. I
also have a much better relationship with my
children and all in all I recommend sobriety.
There will probably always be problems and set
backs however, mainly from others in terms of

family, friends, neighbours and others who will always mistrust me at times and think that the lack of drinking is the actual blip in my life and that I will soon be back with my cans of Special Brew carefully stashed away somewhere, but who the hell cares! If I'm alright, let them think what they like they will anyway with or without any persuasion from me.

Oh! I've not mentioned the fact that I have written this piece of work, which more than anything, has helped me enormously to clarify why I had done certain things and what was due to alcohol and what was just me being a bastard at times, just like the rest of the human race. Being sober hasn't necessarily made me into this great well adjusted person, who goes to church relentlessly every week, no I'm still a prat at times just like the rest of us.

The book has also helped me to get off my arse and use my past nursing and social work experience and my first hand experience of the problems of drink and for me to pass on this knowledge to others. I have now set up a web site, telephone advice line and a one to one counselling service for anyone who wants to give us a try. The organisation is called Empathy :::: Support Services and specialises in advice, counselling and support for people with alcohol related problems. We recognise that it is often a problem which can have a devastating effect on a whole network of other people such as family members, work colleagues and close friends. Often people do not realise the affect alcohol is having on themselves and sometimes prefer to see themselves as a person who can 'handle' themselves and the situation and drink in their minds to solely relax and enjoy themselves.

You may and often do, hold down a responsible

and well paid job and do not relish the thought of other people interfering and talking to anyone whether they are family or friends and least of all your work colleagues about the 'secret' life you lead. You may also realise that your drinking is already out of control and are trying to get to grips with trying to solve the effect it is particularly having on your work situation, family life or many other situations, which at one time you could deal with without any difficulties at all. We cannot profess to be able to 'cure' you, but can show you realistic and practical methods of tackling the various situations you may come across. If you think our service may be able to help you in some way please contact us on the following telephone number: 01484 469030.

Some basic facts about alcohol which may help you, particularly related to the middle aged (like me!)

Alcohol misuse as many of you know, concerns both men and woman, and as can simply be seen by looking at any media coverage, affects people of all ages whether young or old. If you are drinking heavily already and you are only young, sadly you may never reach old or even middle aged. If you are in about your 40s you may be beginning to slow down anyway regardless of whether you have been a heavy drinker since you were young or not. I know through past and present experience that your body just can't take the pounding you once thought was easy to combat, but now you are knackered just trying to keep up with running across a football pitch with your kids. If this is so what chance does that give your kidneys, heart, memory, knee caps…. do I really need to go on?

Yep! lets get real! Like it or not, we are all getting older and will die anyway eventually. Woman and men can all have their face lifts and try and wear their daughters or grand daughters clothes yes ok, or their sons! but we still need to look after ourselves internally, in order to eek out the passing years for as long as possible. One way of helping the process is either stopping drinking if you are as bad as I get with it or at least cut down if you can control it.

The world can be a shit place if you allow it to happen to you through drink so give it your best shot. I do not want to preach to anyone and I won't because I don't deserve to do so, so good luck and thanks for reading my offerings. If they help just one person that is good enough for me. Keep fighting it!

ALCOHOLISM AND BEYOND

Additions to the original book written from 1st May 2006
THE BOOK REVISITED

It is now nearly twelve months since I wrote my first offerings and I have decided it was about time I did an update and also answered some of the questions which I have been met with. I am now doing counselling on a regular basis and have decided to revisit the book and add a few extra pages now that the first print has virtually run out and it seems a shame not to share some of my thoughts. Many people still ask me when I am in the throes of a counselling session or doing a talk to a group, the classic questions I would ask others in the past. 'What exactly made you stop drinking?' and 'was it somebody or something or event that did it for you?' or 'what was the exact time and date when you had your last drink and how did you feel when you knew it was your last drink?'. These questions prompted me to try and develop this book into more of a therapeutic tool, and less of a self history with no real clear answers to the questions posed. 'It's not an easy thing this!' I have told myself on numerous occasions, but here goes anyway!

It may seem like a cop out to some of you that I cannot say that there was an exact time or place when I 'saw the light' and gave up the dreaded curse. There wasn't a light or some new belief that gave me the power to have the strength to do it. Sadly no, it was just bloody hard work over the years and not being put off by the 'blips' as I call them. I admit it! I was too ill physically and mentally to decide I had had enough and the decision was really made for me, either drink and die or abstain and achieve something. I have learnt through counselling others on an individual basis, that every alcoholic has his or her own story to tell and that no two people are exactly alike.

We come from all walks of life with different interests, ages and levels of income and occupations. But we do have some common traits which we would all subscribe to if pressed:

1. We all find good reason for why we drink too much.

2. We all lie, cheat and deceive others when drinking.

3. We all hide drink when we have been found out, unless we have a partner who is also a drinker or is too scared about ruining the relationship he or she has with us.

4. We are usually very clever at planting threats in others and using this to our advantage. 'I will go and live on my own' or 'stop nagging me, you never trust me, I'm off out if you don't shut up' are classic examples of this trait.

5. We all have feelings of the have another drink and 'it won't matter' type.

6. We also have that feeling which is difficult to shift of, 'deserving' and 'counting up brownie points'. We suddenly feel everything is alright and we deserve that drink for doing so well and have been so good for collecting so many points towards it. Then of we go to that offy for a drink.

7. We all forget how hard it was to physically stop drinking and go back to it at the blink of an eye if we don't or someone else doesn't remind us.

8. Just like the drink itself, we all need a quick fix and virtually instant results with no side effects when coming off the alcohol.

9. People try all sorts of things whether it be

acupuncture, relaxation or assertiveness therapy before realising the main element of solving the drink problem is their own inner self wanting to do it and their own will.

10. We have all felt guilty for drinking, ashamed of others knowing and have enjoyed many periods of the drinking before we took it too far.

11. We have all lost a lot through our drinking whether it be money, relationships, houses, jobs or self worth and esteem or, like me, the lot.

12. Many of us end up like me, sick to death of what drinking did to us and having to accept we have lost and drunk away many years of our lives.

13. Many drinkers have to accept they haven't a hope in hell of totally abstaining and don't want to at the moment. However, many people will accept this and will be happy if they could just cut down.

14. Most people find cutting down and not being able to drink as much as they used to do, hard in itself and find relapses back to their old ways almost inevitable at first.

15. Over time, I have talked to many people who have assured me that keeping off the drink has been the right thing to do for them. Some, like

myself, have felt it was not only the right thing to do but also the only alternative they had realistically got. The doctors will tell you in no uncertain terms that only 2% of people make it when they have reached the level of alcohol intake I have described and that you have to keep off it completely to survive, I tend to agree.

DOES COUNSELLING WORK?

For some people, almost certainly yes, for others it is often a very slow process and it is difficult to judge whether you are just their 'latest thing to try' at the end of a long list of other fads they have also tried for a few weeks. Counselling has been seen clearly as a growth industry big time since the 1990s. The British Association of Counselling (BAC) has around 13,000 members, compared with only 600 in 1977. When I was doing my psychiatric nurse training back in 1981, counselling was seen as almost a 'side line' to the main things you could get involved with regarding people. Medication was still the dominant treatment for virtually everything. On some wards, and with specific people, the drugs seemed to work, but for others, all they tended to do was try and mask the symptoms of the illness. Counselling has grown since then and was certainly more apparent when I was completing my Social Work training in the mid nineteen eighties. I suppose I expected it of 'Social Workers' getting you to contemplate your navel and all that 'sort of thing.'

Being trendy, almost now means you should be receiving counselling or therapy, but please don't tell that one to some of the poor bastards I have seen shaking their way across the room.

Ironically, counselling really took off in the 1960's, ironic because it was the period that I personally feel a close affinity with.

Mind you, in the 1960's people as we know, experimented with everything 'man!'

For counselling to work, it is a big commitment for those involved including the alcoholic themselves, their carers and the counselling workers. The counselling work I have done since writing the main part of this book, has involved me working on my own and with my partner Maureen. To date, we have mainly visited people in the privacy of their own homes and on some occasions, they have been to our home. Everyone we have spoken to has preferred the option of choosing where they receive their counselling sessions and a large majority have liked the privacy of their own homes. They can dictate where they sit who they have with them and when the counselling sessions will end. We are not bothered whether they have been drinking five minutes ago just before we arrived as it is their time and money they are wasting if they are not able to take in what we are saying. Most sessions last for an hour, after an initial two hour session. The people we have seen have varied considerably. They have only resembled each other in their need to drink and drink heavily. People have stopped their journey into counselling after buying this book and I have never seen them again, others have moved on a little further and given me a ring having read the book in about one and a half hours. Feedback has included: 'just like our David' and 'It's like you've sat in our living room and watched him for a few years', 'didn't know whether to laugh or cry when I read your book last week'. It was true, I didn't know whether to laugh or cry at these comments. Did they mean the book instilled motivation into them to do something about their drinking or did it drive them to such levels of hopelessness that they would not bother looking any further for further counselling or did they just mean not pursuing further counselling with me? Who knows? But, anyway, as I hear myself saying some people chose to have counselling with me and sometimes with my partner. Each client has been different, with the 'I'm listening to every word your saying' type and the 'I will tolerate you this week, but you must understand I haven't got a problem' type. Some people have used it as a way of appeasing their partner or mum and dad by coming to sessions. These people would usually lie like hell about how much they were drinking and then look relieved when we had finished as though they had passed the 'test'. Clients would often excuse themselves initially, sometimes openly going into the kitchen and downing a bit more vodka to steady the shakes, others were a bit more crafty, at least by going upstairs and taking the bath panel off or the top of the toilet and exposing a half empty bottle of vodka stuck between the ball cock. Most of the time they thought they had succeeded unnoticed, but they forget, I've done exactly the same in the past. This type of behaviour gets them nowhere, and just slows down the process of any recovery. In short, if the person is really committed and does not tell 'porkies' they have a good chance of leading a good life. Counselling is difficult mainly because you cannot show anyone a certificate to say it has worked. We have a tendency in everyday life to weed out the bits of anything we don't like and keep the rest. With group counselling it gets even worse. We as fellow participants have to listen to every body's else's views and stories which may not match our own. I have seen people argue very strongly about a point that I did not necessarily agree with and I am sure I was not alone.

Counselling is a long process and is not an easy fix. Sometimes quite difficult subjects need addressing and I have been asked not to call again on occasions by people who didn't really want to hear the hard and painful truth about themselves. Others expect that even after ten years of hard drinking their son can almost recover overnight through counselling. I'm sorry, but this is not so. It may work in the various documentary filmed, 'boot camps' usually in America, where a snotty nosed fifteen year old runs out of the camp shouting

'I'm sorry mummy, let me hug you!'

In the real world, people have to live where they have always lived and be confronted by the normal problems in life. They do not receive major cash gifts for not drinking and quickly realise that getting off the alcohol itself is the biggest prize they are probably going to receive. Counselling is a two way thing and is not about the counsellor perpetually giving answers to everything.

Most people are well able both physically and psychologically to deal with the many negative physical and mental problems that take place during our lifetime. Family and friends also help us to absorb many such negative events making painless transitions. Deaths, accidents, injuries, loss of loved ones, loss of property, are some common examples of what we have all had to endure at some time during our lives. In addition, there are endless traumas created by us as individuals which usually have a root cause. All these events, whether caused by individuals or natural events, result in the disruption of our normal lives. Some are able to cope with it while others are not. Alcoholism and its effects are almost impossible to cope with for almost everybody. A long process of healing is necessary to bring back the normality in the lives of people who have been exposed to such shit. One of the healing techniques is called counselling.

Counselling can be defined as a therapeutic procedure in which a person (the counsellor) adopts a supportive non- judgmental role to enable a client to deal more effectively with psychological or emotional problems and give advice on some practical and realistic solutions.

A good counsellor is an individual who understands the feelings of the client and treats it as facts, keeps all information in confidence; allows discussion of the issue; builds self esteem of the client; reassures if the client is insecure; solicit the client's own feelings and ideas for a solution. The counsellor will show empathy; show care; have patience; not get distracted during conversation with the client; set goals, build confidence and avoid acting like an expert. Oh!, and have a big ear and a small mouth. In other words LISTEN to what the client and his carers have to say! Your role is not to sit there pretending to listen whilst really spending the whole time just rehearsing what you are going to say next.

A bad counsellor often lacks motivation or any original ideas or solutions; has prejudice against the client and often preconceived notions about the issues facing the client. Sometimes the counsellor may feel a social distance between him self or herself and the client. Most detrimental of all is where the counsellor just isn't really interested in the clients problems and the issues surrounding them.

The person with a drink problem is often a 'dead ringer' of a person needing counselling amongst other things like medical help. A person who is always irritated, angry, distrustful of people, always suspicious, lacks self confidence, always in doubt, in apathy about life, always shows anxiety about the future, resents life and the family, remains isolated, lacks willingness to show any initiative, these are all people who could benefit from counselling.

The main aim of the counsellor is to make the client feel that he/she is able to solve his/her problems on his/her own. There are ten steps to good counselling:

- Encourage the client to talk about their feelings by using good listening skills.
- Use reflective listening
- Let the client let all their grief out.
- Provide missing information about the situation.
- Talk about the client's view of their goals and aspirations in the future.
- Talk about what is needed to get there.
- Look out for signs of trouble and prepare for possible violence or threats.
- Ensure you follow a regular pattern or schedule for follow up meetings and give feedback.
- Always set goals and agree on what steps to take to change the present situation.

Despite the predominance of counsellors and therapists and in fact all other professionals who deal with alcohol issues, there is still a reluctance about seeking help or even admitting you have a problem in the first place so people avoid doing so. People try a lot of other things to 'try and do something about it'. People have tried distraction (to try and cheer themselves up), avoidance (in the hope that it will just go away or get better or it is just too painful to confront), or suffer in silence.

For me counselling works better listening to what others have to say and giving some advice about what a person could do if they want to, in the future. As well as having a background in psychiatric nursing and social work I have first hand experience of going through all the trials and tribulations of being an alcoholic myself and combating its mysteries, hopefully. Those who provide empathic support at times of crises are crucial to our future well being, and this is particularly so with somebody suffering from alcohol problems. On the whole, I feel that counselling can work rather than using the term 'does work,' but as I keep saying, it is only yet another tool for you bag of tricks and it is only yourself who can beat it.

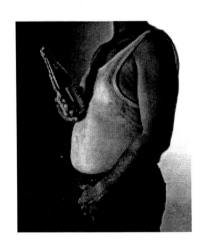

'IT IS ONLY YOU WHO CAN BEAT IT'.

BINGE DRINKING

'There were now't like that when I were a lad, supping were for blokes not snotty nosed little kids. Men deserved it when the'd spent all day in't mill
with all that dust and that. Today its all changed, young kids ride around on their bikes, hanging out of the windows of dodgy cars with two litre bottles of cider at their throats. Come Monday morning, there back at school or in some tuppence ha'penny job acting as though butter wouldn't melt in their mouths'.

The beauty of growing up! To most people, this type of drinking is purely for young free and easy teenagers. It brings to mind a self destructive and unrestrained type of person who sets off on a bender every so often. They go at it hell for leather for a couple of days and during this time they drop out of going to work, say to hell with any of their responsibilities, blow all their money, beat the hell out of somebody and finish off with some bird or bloke up a back alley!
But is it really, as the newspapers often say to us,

a new phenomena that only relates to young people?

In my time, as a more than too old law student I have mixed with many people both male and female who would fit the binge drinking definition. People who were sound hard working people during the day, most of the time, who would suddenly get the urge to chill out and in short, get absolutely pissed very quickly. I'm not really bothered about studying the various statistics which are constantly banded around. I prefer to look at the people I have seen both as a psychiatric nurse and as a counsellor and alcoholic myself.

Many of the so called binge drinkers I have come across, do so not because they are necessarily an alcoholic at the moment, although they could be heading that way. A lot of kids of an average age of around fourteen have hung around off licences for years. They do it for something to do and meet their mates. If they are lucky they may be able to scrounge a few cigs or even better, collar some sucker to go into the shop and blag them a bottle of cider and ten cigs. When I was of a similar age I did the same sort of thing. We would wait until our parents went on holiday or even better somebody else's mum and dad, then blow all our money on cigs and beer. In the early 1970s, it was all party 7's and fizzy Youngers Tartan Bitter and we were happily pissed in no time. We would drink as fast as we could to get pissed and I don't think this trend has changed.

Today though, it has a number of different elements to it. Binge drinking also includes adults with enough money to do it properly without having to ask some poor sod sat on a bench outside the off licence to help you to buy it. So called 'professionals' do it on a weekend in the same way as those kids on their bikes. Barbeques happen all the time and it appears to legitimise the 'old get together and lets get pissed for the next two days type attitude'.

Even though alcohol is legal for those over a certain age, there is no getting away with it, it is a harmful, dangerous drug at times. It can appear that everyone drinks and that everyone drinks a lot, but look a little bit closer....... what a load of crap!

There are loads of people who don't drink at all

and a lot of people who don't drink heavily.

People tend to kid themselves that it is chill out time and it is all a bit of fun and games, but try and convince those affected by your antics. Do they think it is funny when you puke three foot away from the bog and can't quite muster enough energy to clean it up until you have just about sobered up. Lets face it, these type of drinkers might not yet be alcoholics, but they sure as hell make a good effort at mimicking the same symptoms.

Binge drinkers:

- Drink to get pissed. They aim to get blathered and lose any form of self control. Ask any seasoned alcoholic, we have all done it. Unfortunately, a person can't just lose control of the bits of his or her body and retain the rest. 'I think I will have a bit of confidence and be the life and sole of that wedding I am the best man at next week'. I'm afraid not! The bloke sways at the alter, whilst trying to hold on to his breakfast and makes a right prick of himself at his wedding speech.

- They drink large quantities and drink

quickly to get the buzz or bum's rush they want so badly.

- They do stupid things, most commonly drinking and driving, sometimes at the same time. If you are concerned about someone drinking too much even if you don't think they are an alcoholic, just have a look in the glove compartment of their car or the works van. Does it just contain a half eaten Mars bar or is there something a bit more sinister lurking? Do they begin to argue or begin to appear 'over happy' all of a sudden, just when they have returned from the shops for that 'extra loaf of bread' you didn't particularly want anyway.

The sensible non binge drinker, doesn't drink and drive and doesn't drink to get drunk. They may like the taste of the drink and may be after a mild relaxing effect but they stop drinking before they feel 'drunk'. They drink less and drink far more slowly having food with it.

There are a number of disparities regarding the amount of alcohol you need to drink in order for you to 'qualify' as the session being a 'binge'.

One of the most commonly used thresholds for 'binge' drinking is five or more drinks for men and four for woman, per session. However, its about as accurate as 'how long is a piece of string' in my eyes. In today's age of Super Strength beer amongst other things, who the hell really knows what counts as a 'binge'. One explanation of 'binge' drinking is characterised by the consumption of alcohol until total intoxication usually alone and lasting for a few days and resulting in a loss of control.

The British Medical Association concludes that 'in common usage, binge drinking is now usually used to refer to heavy drinking over an evening or similar time span and is sometimes also referred to as heavy episodic drinking.

In most of Europe, children and adolescents routinely experience alcohol much earlier than say America, and often with the approval of their parents. The drinking age in most countries is eighteen and younger people can often buy alcohol in certain settings, such as in a restaurant with their parent's supervision. Parents may also choose to provide drinks such as diluted wine or beer mixed with lemonade with a meal to encourage responsible drinking. For example, the legal age for drinking and buying beer in Denmark, Germany, Austria and The Netherlands is sixteen years of age.

In the United Kingdom, we know that many newspapers devote a lot of their time talking about the 'social ills' of our present society, that is getting worse by the day according to some. This notion is also repeated in television programmes and the news in general, with pictures of a bedraggled woman staggering up the street with a bottle of something clasped in her hands. To try and tackle the problems the government has introduced a number of measures to deter disorderly behaviour and the sales of alcohol to those under eighteen. In January 2005, it was reported that there were one million admissions to Accident And Emergency Departments which were alcohol related. In 2005, the Licensing Act 2003 came into effect in the United Kingdom, partly intended to tackle binge drinking. Personally, however, I only think it will make matters worse, especially with the start of twenty four hour licensing.

The culture of drinking in the United Kingdom is very different to that carried out in other countries, but is very similar to that shown in the Republic of Ireland. In mainland Europe, people tend to drink more slowly over an evening with a meal. In the U.K. alcohol is drunk at an entirely different pace and without a great deal of food, except when we are at the now great British trend of barbeques. Usually at barbeques there is at least one or two people who will be going hell for leather through the cans of Stella and it is seen as socially acceptable to many. Usually a person is only 'found out' as being a big drinker when they fall over the barbeque or as has happened to me, fell in it!

It is acknowledged that, particularly amongst young people, it is often seen as socially unacceptable to remain sober at such times. Alcoholics have told me that the reason they don't really go out any more is because of the pressures of their mates to 'have a drink'. One person told me of the times he had told his mum that he thought he had a problem, only to be greeted with a fridge full of cans at his mums and told to go out for a drink with her family, which he deserved for keeping off the beer for a few days!

Alcohol is very slowly being seen as a serious problem by the media and politicians. It is unfair in my view to attribute all the bad behaviour to anyone who drinks a few on a night out, but it doesn't help matters, as my experience has shown me. Keeping your alcohol consumption low can be boring at times but it sure as hell stops or slows down many of the problems you will face if you get a few years of heavy drinking under your belt.

QUESTIONS AND ANSWERS

Have you ever wanted to get some quick answers to specific questions which you didn't always get the chance to ask at the time? The following, are my answers to some of the key questions I have been asked about alcoholism either as comments about the book I have written, talks I have given, attendance at alcohol groups and private individual counselling sessions. Of course, it also includes my own personal experiences and what I would have liked to have known at the time. At the end of the book I have written some contact numbers for organisations which cover the North of England, but please ask your doctor where is the best place for you. If there are other organisations it is worthwhile me including, please let me know.

Regarding the answers to the questions, I cannot profess that they are the best and right answers, or the answers people have wanted to hear, but they are about me and my experiences and not just what I have read in books about the subject. They have often been asked by people desperate for a definitive answer in order to get to grips with their problem or a relative or friend:

Q. What the hell caused me to start drinking and when did I turn into an alcoholic?

A. Good question, most of the people I have talked to have grappled with this one, sometimes for a number of years. People can often not remember when they first realised they had a problem with alcohol. It is usually a very slow process. People more often than not, start as a social drinker, drinking the same as everyone else and gradually build up the amount they are drinking. They like the 'buzz' it is giving them and enjoy that 'bums rush' sensation of one minute feeling tense and tired and the next feeling as though all their worries have melted away. The feeling is great whilst no one is seeing it as a problem and you are holding down a job and you have never been in trouble with the police, neighbours, your family or work colleagues. But this does not last for ever, inevitably this bubble of security and release will burst and the shit does hit the fan.

Q. How will I know I have reached rock bottom?

A. Unfortunately you may not know. It is such a slow and insidious process. People I have met have lost everything through drinking and I mean everything! From being a happy go lucky male or female with a good job and as they saw it, a happy marriage, they have systematically lost their job, got divorced, got in trouble with the police, blacked out, been in hospital and so on and so forth and still the message hasn't clicked and they carry on drinking not realising most people would judge them as being at rock bottom. Perhaps this is the answer, other people need to tell you the lift has stopped, you have in fact landed in that big pile and it doesn't smell that good.

Q. When will I start to feel better?

A. Stopping drinking is one hell of a thing to do and without the risk of repeating myself too many times, you have to want to do it for yourself and not necessarily to please others. If you just want to please others you won't do it I can assure you. You will probably feel worse rather than better at first. After the first euphoric feelings of managing to physically overcome the withdrawal symptoms the real work begins. What the hell can I do with my time? and why isn't everybody acknowledging how well I have done? Unfortunately life isn't that simple. If you are constantly looking for praise from others you may be disappointed. I spent months wondering why people didn't pat me on the back and say well done you have beaten it! The wiser folk around you will realise that it is not a case of stopping for a few weeks. One or two scary trips to hospital can assist in the process. However, not where you were virtually forced to stop drinking in some nice plush hospital setting where you could sleep all day or attend an optional encounter group. This is the real world! Where people aren't as kind as when you were 'dying' in hospital. Many people realise that this is the same person who lied and cheated their way through your money and upset basically everyone around them eventually. It takes time to shift those views but when they do you should start to feel better. You don't necessarily feel better in a 'haven't I done well kind of way' but more in a private self worth kind of way, which believe you me, is much more worthwhile.

Q. When will others start to begin to trust me again?

A. When they are sure you can be trusted. This, for people who don't see you very often may be years for others it may be a matter of months.
No amount of persuasion or action will stop people mistrusting you it is just a matter of time. One of the hardest things for people to get their heads round is why it can take so long for people to trust you again. You have to have an acceptance of it, in order to get on with your future.

Q. When did you realise this was going to be your last drink?

A. For me personally, I had been so ill with drinking that I cannot remember when I last literally had a drink but I know when I began feeling that I had had enough. It is apparently one and a half years ago, although I refuse to count the days. For other people, they seem to be able to remember the exact time, date, place and what they were drinking at the time they gave up, ah well each to their own.

Q. What about the blips you mention in the book?

A. Blips as I describe them, are really short relapses back to drinking again, but if handled properly are not a fully blown session which for me could last for several weeks. I have talked to many people about blips and was given numerous interpretations of what we mean by them and what to do about them. One person described them as the sort of situation when you have no intention of entering a pub and might just drive past one and as you do so you get the urge to go in. A couple of hours later you are blathered and have no money left, you leave the car and walk home. Which ever way you try and rationalise this behaviour you will have to do something about it. You have two choices you can either wallow in your own shit and bugger on steady again drinking or stop again. If it is a 'one off' you can sober up quite quickly and get on with just abstaining if it is a longer session you may need medical help again but just do it! Feelings of guilt are part and parcel of the process of getting off it again but are worth it. One of the key themes of this book is to learn how to accept yourself and not be plagued by constant internal criticism: putting it another way, try and begin to feel at ease with yourself. A key factor in doing this is to put your mistakes into perspective. Do not dwell too heavily on the fact you were doing so well with your drinking and now feel very low because you have 'broken your duck'. Just learn something from your mistake and don't carry on drinking.

Q. How long will it take before I can be sure I have beaten it?

A. You will probably never know for sure. The best you can do is stop drinking completely or cut down as much as you can. However, you will always have times when you feel like a drink or think you have beaten it for a short time. There is a need to accept your lot and realise that the problem remains with you but you can manage and enjoy yourself like you used to do. The trick is not to dwell on the facts of your prolonged drinking and enjoy other things in life. Drink is often linked with having a good time and giving you the confidence to do so. However this doesn't last and you can soon feel low in mood and downright depressed if you start drinking again. Try imagining yourself feeling fit and well on a hot summers day and you are thirsty- if you cannot resist and have a strong craving for alcohol you know you have still not got it under control.

Q. Will I ever be able to drink again, once I am fit and well?

A. No, not if you want to be sure you can remain off it. Feeling fit and well can often make us forget we were very ill and up until a very short time ago, extremely drunk and incapable of doing very much. Once you begin to drink again you run the risk of it getting worse and worse every day you continue. Remember, very few people once in the throes of alcoholism, can ever successfully recover to such an extent to where they can comfortably drink again without ending up back where they started again. Of course like I always say, its up to you.

Q. Do you feel able to walk into a pub and not have a drink now?

A. Yes I do, and I do, if that makes sense. I sometimes go to the local pub which is the only one which would have me in the end when I was drinking! At first it was difficult facing other people and trying to pretend I was interested in what they were saying when they were drunk, but after a few months this was reduced to a certain extent by me only going out with a few friends rather than trying to take the whole pub with me. I mainly drink cokes in the pub and people don't bother or pester me at all.

Q. What is it like to see other people pissed or enjoying themselves?

A. Far from being a bad experience, I now find it quite funny at times. I have watched people turn from being a quiet spoken, supposedly 'sensible' and 'well adjusted' person turn into a loud mouthed blithering wreck with the drink and then just puke it up all over themselves.

Most people enjoying themselves, is a matter of degree, initially after a few pints they are fine, but any more and they begin to lose it. There are varying types of people who emerge as different personalities once under the influence. Firstly, there's John Travolta man. He will dance to anything and try and get everybody else up to watch him. Enough said on this personality, I think you will know who I mean. Secondly, there's Mr. Advice man, who and despite not doing that well at school, has managed to turn into the most knowledgeable man in the world. He or she can and does advise you on everything! Then there is Mr. Quite, the man who is usually very quiet and then suddenly sees the light when he has had a few lagers, everybody is wonderful and the person next to him is always in need of another drink. I could go on, but I am boring myself now. Anyway, back to the question, no, I am not bothered about other people enjoying themselves whilst out drinking and I do not have to hide in the toilets with another person with his or her hidden vodka bottle.

Q. Is there a cure for alcoholism?

A. There is no known cure for alcoholism, although alcoholism can be treated. In other words, even if an alcoholic has been sober for a long time and has regained his or her health, they remain susceptible to relapse and must continue to avoid alcohol. 'Cutting down' on drinking doesn't always work and sometimes there is a need to cut out alcohol completely for a successful recovery.

Q. Why do I always feel depressed? does the alcohol cause this?

A. Alcohol the drug is a depressant. It is a central nervous system depressant. I'm not surprised you feel depressed. That is why it is no use taking anti- depressant medication and drinking alcohol at the same time. There are a number of ways in which alcohol and depression may be linked and hopefully the chapter below may give you a further insight. To get a bit technical which I usually prefer to avoid, at the level of brain chemistry we know that alcohol directly interferes with some of the brain mechanisms for regulating mood, sleep and appetite. On the social side of things life can be stressful at times for everybody and can lead to drinking too much and depression.

Q. Everybody else drinks as much as me, so why is it me who is having to come for counselling?

A. Usually people go through a stage of thinking they are alright and it is everybody else who has the problem with drinking. The drinking is usually found out by a partner or friend finding bottles or cans hidden neatly in cupboards in the house or in the bushes or plant pots near to the house. People often don't see they have a problem if others around them are drinking just as much as them. What the person doesn't realise is that their 'mate' isn't quite drinking as much and isn't drinking before they both set off out to the pub like they are doing or are not drinking every night.

Some people can drink every night and habitually do so and show little in terms of long term effects. However, that is what we know, some people may not be drinking as much as we think, just like we are drinking too much. You have to decide for yourself what are the limits for you, other people can only guide you.

Q. Do some people ever deny they have a drink problem?

A. Yes they do! Most people deny they even drink too much never mind have a problem with it. For example, I recently visited a man, who was living alone having been drinking and driving and was not able to work. He had lost his job and his partner had left him. He ended up in hospital and was on life support for some weeks. He told everybody he had just fallen over his cat and banged his head, apart from this he was O.K. and didn't know what the problem was. This is an extreme example of denial and was probably not a lie in his eyes. He had literally forgotten what had happened to him. Most people have a certain level of denial because the truth can hurt. Often, it is not until someone loses something like a job, a partner or something else which is important to them before they realise they have a problem. For the majority of people I have met, they have often lost a lot before anybody has become involved to help them. They then spend a lot of their time and energy on thinking what could have been. However, every time this type of situation arises because of drink the person takes little notice until it is too late.

Q. What drinks are strong and which should I avoid. I want to cut down on my drinking and don't want to drink any silly stuff?

A. This is a very practical question which is asked by everybody I have ever talked to.. Total abstinence is probably going to give you the best chance of keeping on top of it, but we have to accept that cutting down is the next best thing. In all honesty it is the only thing we can achieve for some, life would be so miserable for the person if they could not have just a small drink. In addition, if you stop drinking too quickly you could have withdrawal effects. If you genuinely just want to cut down, then do it gradually. Keep a diary of the amount you are drinking. Also the number of units this adds up to; how much you spent on the alcohol and how you felt just before you drank and how you felt just after. Also try and describe how you felt two hours later. The following may help you with the units of alcohol.

Drinks can be very deceiving for a novice drinker at sixteen or so you think it is good just to get served in a pub never mind what the alcohol content is! We tend to drink at first anything which tastes like something we are used to, like fizzy pop and brightly coloured liquid as long as it is cheap. As we move on in our drinking career we are a bit choosier and tend to go for something that will give us a buzz but not make us throw up everywhere. Later on we will drink anything if we have got hooked on it and the cheaper the better.

Alcoholics need to drink cheaply to survive, particularly if you have spent your dole cheque, this is how we end up drinking 'White Lightning' or practically anything with the words 'White' in the title. Or we go for my old favourite, Special Brew and stick it in the fridge for a while before we drink it. The strong ciders are probably the worst drinks you can have, for being almost too cheap and full of chemicals. My mate once said to me:

'your not drinking that stuff are you? You would be better siphoning your petrol tank!'

To get an idea of the possible effects of alcohol and what you can expect to happen to you depending on what your tolerance level is. The imaginary person I am referring to, has not built up or developed a tolerance to alcohol:

An average person may get a blood alcohol concentration of 50 mg/dL after two drinks drunk quickly. Their condition is likely to deteriorate in the following way:

50 mg = two pints of normal beer, you my feel a warmth, have skin which is flushed; impaired judgement and decreased inhibitions.

100 mg/dL = an obvious intoxication in most people with an increased impairment of judgement, inhibition, attention, and control;

Some impairment of muscular performance; and a slowing down of your reflexes.

150 mg/dL = an obvious intoxication in all normal people. Staggering gait and other muscular lack of co-ordination; slurred speech; double vision; memory and comprehension loss.

250 mg/dL = Extreme intoxication or stupor, reduced response to stimuli, inability to stand, vomiting, incontinence and sleepiness

350 mg/dL = A coma, unconsciousness, little response to stimuli, incontinence, low body temperature, poor respiration, fall in blood pressure, clammy skin.

500 mg/dL = death likely

Q. Is Alcoholism a disease?

A. Yes. Alcoholism is a chronic and often progressive disease with symptoms that include a strong need to drink despite the proof of such negative consequences, such as serious job or health related problems. Like many diseases, it has generally a predictable course of action with very recognisable symptoms. It is influenced by genetic and environmental factors which continue to be pretty much well defined.

Q. What could go wrong medically?

A. Many people have asked me this question and I often say nothing much if you stop drinking and a great deal if you don't. This is where the involvement of your doctor at an early stage is necessary just to get a 'benchmark' of where you are at at the moment. Many people go to their doctors too late and their liver for example, is packing up. You need to get in there and sort out what maybe available to you if needed in the future. It is of little use waiting until your relative or friend is in need of detox and you are having to wait days or weeks for a place in a clinic. I may sound pessimistic, but, sort out the information you have available at an early stage and not just before you get into a taxi with your son holding onto you for dear life.

The alcohol can effect you both physically and

mentally and your doctor is the person to see. He will almost certainly ask for tests on your liver which just means him taking a little bit of blood, but obviously other tests maybe asked for as he takes down your history. I have talked to many people who have been very scared and put off by even the thought of any tests even though they knew something may be wrong. Many people including my self, didn't want to know the results and were happier to continue drinking, this is and was a big mistake. The relationship between drinking and your health is a complex issue. Alcohol is related to over sixty different medical conditions. Heavy drinking can increase the risks for certain cancers, especially those of the liver, oesophagus, throat, and larynx (voice box). The liver gets the arse end of the damage but like I have mentioned above most organs can be affected. To put it bluntly, alcohol is strictly a poison, which our liver manages to 'detoxify'. Excess alcohol inflames the cells, causing hepatitis, as a result of which the drinker becomes jaundiced and he or she basically looks yellow including their eyes. Prolonged abuse leads to scarring of the liver, which is eventually called 'cirrhosis' - in which much of the liver is replaced by useless scar tissue. In short, and I can't put it in any form or nicer way, yes, it will cause an early death.

Q. If my son is drinking a lot, could it be something to do with his father who was always drinking?

A. There is little if any evidence of a straight genetic link between an alcoholic and one of his or her children, but if that person is susceptible to drink and is almost surrounded by it all the time, they have a much greater chance of becoming an alcoholic themselves. Alcoholism is a chronic disease with a mixture of genetic, psychosocial and environmental factors influencing its development.

On saying the above, there is evidence of links between generations. There is something called Foetal Alcoholic Syndrome, or damage caused to babies of mothers who drink during pregnancy.

Q. What is this 'sweet tooth' thing that I have just read about on the internet?

A. A bloke called Alexy Kampov - Polevoy and his colleagues at the University of North Carolina School of Medicine in the U.S. have recently announced a major review of recent studies into the links between diet preferences and drinking patterns. They have come up with the conclusion that your tendency to be an alcoholic can be predicted from your diet. Quite simply, people who prefer sweet foods as opposed to not sweet, as they refer to them, have, yes you've guessed it, a 'sweet tooth' and are much more inclined to have alcoholic tendencies. There now appears to be a genetic link between the preference for sweet tastes and the genetic predisposition to drink too much alcohol. Alcoholics tend to have a sweet tooth, and those who prefer the sweetest of foods have the strongest hereditary component to their alcoholism. Those trying to break their addiction and dependency, have found that eating much more sugary foods than usual can stop or stem the craving for a drink. In short watch what you eat!

Q. Is it as bad as drugs for getting you hooked on it?

A. Yes it is.

Alcohol is often not thought of as a drug, probably just because most people cannot cope without it. It is commonly used for both religious and social purposes throughout the world. It is a drug, however, and compulsive drinking has become one of society's most serious problems.

There is no doubt about it, drink as in alcohol is addictive. It is something your body becomes accustomed to and in time begins to rely on it to survive. You in effect become dependent on the habit which is either physically or mentally or both. Remember alcohol is a drug in itself just like cannabis or cocaine. Alcohol is a substance also called ethanol which is the most psychoactive substance used after caffeine.

Chronic alcohol intake is associated with several degenerative and inflammatory processes in the central nervous system and can produce a depressor effect. In short this is why many people drink to get rid of their depression and just feel worse afterwards. When you feel like a drink remember you are drinking ethanol. Sounds a bit more like a drug now doesn't it!

Q. I'm thinking of sending him to one of those private clinics, I know it will cost me but I want the best.

A. Right, and so you should want the best, but private clinics are not always the best answer just because of the price. The type of treatment you receive and its benefits often depend on the severity of the alcoholism and the resources available in your community. A clinic may look wonderful and your son or partner may have all the benefits of a nice room with nice bedding and a T.V. and telephone, but is it all gearing him up for the real world? In the early stages of recovery it may seem fine but what about in a few weeks time when he is still lounging in the spa and not going to any group therapy sessions because he would rather stay in his room and watch his plasma T.V.? Treatment may include detoxification which is the process of safely getting alcohol out of your system, taking medication prescribed by your doctor and of course counselling. Many of these services are provided on an out-patient basis and do not necessarily require a hospital admission. You should seek medical advice from your doctor as to whether an admission to a clinic is really necessary. I ended up in a cycle of admission, after admission to various hospitals which were both run privately and by the Health Service. They did detoxify me and I began to feel physically well, but they did not change my mental state and so I just carried on drinking after a few days of discharge. Obviously, a hospital or clinic admission is sometimes necessary to ensure you do not have severe withdrawal effects. Ask your local G.P. regarding the local services and costs and most importantly, waiting times. Get yourself prepared just in case that family member needs the services at the last minute.

Q. All his mates go out drinking every night and so is he just following what their doing?

A. Like all of us we will follow others at times,

all be it sometimes subconsciously. We do it right from the school playground age where we follow what type of football boots our friends are wearing and this continues throughout our lives. We follow are friends in pubs and copy what they are drinking to be socially acceptable and we don't like being the odd one out. Unfortunately for some people, our drinking becomes too much of a habit, and over a period we can become so addicted to it that it is impossible for us to break the habit at the time.

Being 'socially acceptable' and a good fun type of person falls on its arse when the drinking gets out of hand. Far too often I have heard people tell me they can 'handle it'. A few months later they are out of work. It doesn't matter how many times you warn people about the social effects of drinking too much, the same predictable effects often happen. Alcohol, as my story to date will tell you, more often than not leads to problems at work in the form of absenteeism, sickness and under-performance, and other colleagues begin to see this happening. It is not just the smell on your breath, which often gets worse throughout the day not better, but your general self is noticeably different. A client I was seeing said that his workmates would often think he had been drinking heavily the night before, but fail to realise its was the cans he had drunk before arriving at work that made his breath smell and was making him more and more agitated as the day progressed. Very often, the person gets sacked, not for being profoundly pissed whilst at work, but because like all things, good and bad, word gets round and you build up a reputation for being a drinker. Jobs which you were trusted to do are taken away from you more and more, until you are finally taken into that office for the start of a 'capability study.' Excessive alcohol intake also increases contact with the police through driving offences, drunk and disorderly behaviour or violent crime. In short, doing 'what your mates do' is O.K. but believe you me, they will drop you like a ton of bricks if you end up out of work with marital problems and no money!

Q. He pissed the bed on Saturday night, is this normal?

A. Unfortunately yes it is, if the person has drunk

too much. Continued heavy drinking can cause both loss of bladder control and your bowel movement control (I should know !) These can be reversed by abstinence from alcohol. Alcohol is what you call a diuretic , which causes the bladder to fill quickly, and this usually triggers the need to urinate quickly and often. Alcohol can also impair the ability to know when to urinate and do it in the right place at the right time!

Q. He is hiding cans everywhere, should I let him know I keep searching for them?

A. He will probably already know you have been looking for empty bottles or cans, tackling him regarding this will only annoy him even more. He or she has to take responsibility for their own actions which includes what happens to the cans. If they keep hiding them, let them, and just casually tell them every so often to clear up the mess of empty cans. Most people hide the cans for a number of reasons. Firstly, they don't want anyone else to know that they are drinking so much, secondly, they don't want reminding of it, and lastly they don't want the cans and bottles taking away from them. An alcoholic often builds up fears of running out of alcohol and then not being able to cope with its effects. It is of little use telling a person off for drinking and much better to gradually let them open up with the answers and be truthful with you.

Q. What is all this 12 step recovery thing all about?

A. 'Twelve- steppers usually meet once a week in a church or school all purpose room or other public area. In these meetings, members commonly discuss issues such as what led them down the path to alcoholism and what made them seek help. The members of the program will support those who are in trouble and applaud those who are doing well or are 'victorious'. Many of these meetings open with prayer. The rest of the meeting will include personal stories of different members of the program.

The 'twelve steps' refer to the steps a recovering alcoholic must take to overcome his or her addiction as part of this program. The first step is to admit you have a problem. Whilst the steps may be different for each addiction or compulsion the 'twelve step' program tries to deal with, the idea is the same. Besides admitting your addiction, members also have to own up to their past mistakes and make any necessary amends. This may mean saying sorry to anyone the alcoholic has hurt in the past. Most 'twelve step' programs are spiritual in nature. Although God is mentioned often in the twelve steps, they are not considered to be religious programs. Members are required however, to seek help from a higher power and atone (make amends) for their sins. In addition to encouraging an alcoholic to admit problems and make amends, twelve-step programs also encourage members to regain control of their lives and offer solutions and emotional support so they will avoid future temptation. Twelve step programs aren't considered rehabilitation. Instead they are considered 'recovery' programs, as in recovering your life.

Q. What about me as a carer? What help can I get?

A. Many professionals now advocate the whole

family being involved in the care of the person with the drink problem. Sometimes, the carers have their own specialised group they can attend and talk through issues. As a relative or friend of a long term drinker, you will have suffered a lot and may well have reached the point of not feeling you are able to open yourself up to the very likely hurt and trauma of getting involved yet again. You may remember washing your hands of the matter and 'getting a life again' on numerous occasions. However, for anyone seeking recovery from alcoholism, how their family reacts to them is vital to them both before, during and after any treatment they receive.

Any doctor, clinic or counsellor worth their salt will spend a great deal of time with you, giving advice of what to do and say when you are confronted with different situations.

Q. How do you feel now and are you ever tempted to have a drink?

A. I do not have a physical or mental desire to drink anymore. When I think of drink I can only think of all the negatives which were involved for me, like puking, headaches hospital, thinking I was going to die and others thinking I was going to as well, no I don't miss drinking anymore. Don't get me wrong, I have in the past thought about drink, but that was as far as it got. I can now enjoy simply sitting on my front steps or reading a book in peace and without looking over my shoulder in case another policeman or ambulance turns up and I have forgotten what I have done.

Q. What exactly do we mean by 'detox'

A. Again, a good question which is important to understand but a fairly simple process, if it goes alright. 'Detox' is merely getting rid of all the alcohol in the body or detoxification of it. It is a method of helping someone to come off alcohol safely and involves stopping all alcohol intake. It is usually helped by doctors prescribing medication such as diazepam (Valium) or chlordiazepoxide (Librium). Sometimes people are lucky and just have a bad headache and flu like symptoms and a bit of feeling sick, at the other end of the scale people can end up with very bad withdrawal symptoms particularly if they give up drinking too quickly. These symptoms include, fits, hallucinations, and terrible tremors of the hands for example. If people run the risk of being this bad, they probably need hospital care until these symptoms subside. In my opinion, once a person is out of the physical danger period of alcohol, he or she is best having therapy back at home rather than remaining in a medical environment when mental intervention is what is needed. For many of the above reasons, serious alcohol withdrawal is dangerous particularly if not left in the care of the medical profession. It should always be done, with medical help at hand whether the treatment is carried out at home or in a hospital setting.

Q. What do people mean when they say they have had 'DTs'?

A. It is short for delirium tremens, and like all the other side effects you may suffer from like tremor, anxiety, restlessness, sweating, nausea, seizures (fits) when you come off alcohol, this is just another one. DTs only seem to effect about 5%

of all the people withdrawing from alcohol, but it is serious believe you me. When I fell off that hospital trolley I mentioned earlier in the book, had a fit and ended up in 'resuss'. I think you get the general picture of what I'm talking about. Complications such as dehydration, fits and pneumonia can occur. It happens three days or so after stopping drinking and can last for up to seven days. The symptoms are those of withdrawal and disorientation (being unaware of where you are, what time, day or year it is, and who other people are), seeing or hearing things that are not there) and delusions (having false beliefs, especially being frightened of certain situations and people. Think back to my earlier chapters about me thinking I was in the S.A.S. for example, and my daughter talking about me, thinking I was in a bombing raid in our local park!

Q. Do you feel happy all the time, now you have got off the alcohol?

A. No I don't, in all honesty, and I don't think any one does, whether they drink or not, but I do feel happier now and I have regained some of my dignity and the trust of others. I also relax a lot more because I don't have the thoughts in the back of my mind that I will die because of pointless alcohol consumption in the future. I also never want to have those terrible withdrawal effects again or permanently being in debt and selling anything for more alcohol. Abstinence does not cure everything and you often revert to being what you were before you drunk too much and that's O.K. by me.

ALCOHOL AND DEPRESSION

Many people I have met, have mentioned the feelings of being low in mood or quite simply feeling very depressed. I felt the same way for years and I mentioned earlier in the book about seeing my doctor about getting some medication to cure it. But what the hell is it?

Depression is a common and serious illness for some, I learnt this very quickly whilst working in psychiatric nursing. I nursed a 'no nonsense' farmer once in hospital and was told to 'special him'. This merely meant following him around everywhere to make sure he didn't do anything 'silly'. He went to the toilet and I followed, but gave him the dignity of opening his bowels in his cubicle alone. After a few minutes I knocked on the door, there was no reply, he had hung himself using his pyjama cord on the hook at the back of the door.

There is often wide spread misunderstanding of depression with people shrugging it of as 'not a real illness'.

Symptoms of depression include feeling

'worthless' and 'useless' rather than feeling 'ill' and as for getting better this is reduced to hopeless and sometimes a clear belief that nothing will help.

I am sure everybody has heard the expression, 'pull yourself together' or 'its all in your mind'. Of course it bloody is! that's the problem. Both carers and sufferers alike battle with these sorts of questions and statements day after day. The consequences are, that, just like that bloke who hung himself, sometimes seriously ill people do not get or look for the help they need.

This chapter is about those questions that both carers and alcoholics ask, including why it is not possible to simply 'pull yourself together'.

Depression is one of the most common conditions that Joe public ever gets affected by, so how come when you look round a supermarket or other people on the bus you have no chance of picking out those people who are depressed? Granted, the same could be said of many medical conditions which are not very clear and obvious to the man in the street. If you ask everybody in a hall to put up their hands if they feel they suffer from bad colds or hay fever you would probably get a big response, but try seeing how many people will put up their hands and shout 'I am a depressed person'

We don't like to talk about mental illness in general and its about as low down the league table as saying you are an alcoholic or have a drink problem.

There are some common symptoms to depression:

- Low in mood
- Inability to get any pleasure out of things that were normally pleasurable
- Loss of interest in almost everything
- Feeling tired all the time, with no energy
- Difficulty sleeping
- Eating very little and not being interesting in food.
- Going up and down in weight, sometimes 'comfort eating,' then not eating at all.
- Feeling tense, restless and anxious.
- Losing self confidence and avoiding other people.
- Being irritable and losing the will to concentrate on any thing for very long.
- Finding it harder and harder to make

decisions which at one time you would have found easy.

- Feeling guilty, useless and inadequate.
- For many, the feelings of suicide.

As many of us know too well, the feelings mentioned above, do not affect everybody in the same way or at the same times. With all that said, there is one thing I am absolutely certain of, all the symptoms of depression can be brought about by alcohol consumption. You can certainly reduce your chances of having depressive episodes by keeping off or lowering your alcohol intake. Alcohol is involved in the cause of many car crashes and suicides as mentioned earlier. It doesn't take much working out to realise that many of these people were 'on a downer' and drank because of this or as a result of this. Alcohol is estimated to be involved in about thirty per cent of all suicides and plays a particularly large role in adolescent suicide and in suicide with the use of firearms; and it is highly associated with homicides.

Nearly all the people both male and female I have had dealings with as a nurse, social worker or as a counsellor in the past, have all had bouts of tearfulness feeling worthless and the rest. Personally, as I think I have already mentioned, I did the usual thing of going to the doctors for medication and blamed it all on being depressed. I even drank to give myself 'a lift' from my dark miserable life. Did I drink to make myself happier or was it the drink that in the first place made me feel sad? I think I know the answer now.

During drinking spells, about 40% of heavy drinkers would fit the description of depression I have mentioned, but when they are on the wagon they have the same rates of depression as the rest of the population.

In addition, about 5-10% of depressed people have many of the symptoms of an alcohol problem. There is no doubt about it in my mind people use alcohol and get pissed especially as a way of escaping reality, in the same way as I have described my self in earlier chapters. Alcohol can for a short time, (which gets shorter and shorter) believe me, give you a pleasant and relaxed feeling, so people use it as a means of escape and to get away from unhappy thoughts and feelings of divorce, money problems and so on.

Alcohol can also make you fall asleep much more easily, as I found out on occasions when I fell asleep on the bog in my local. The only trouble is, the type of sleep it induces, is crap and it certainly used to make me feel even worse or at least just as tired as if I hadn't had bothered. I ended up needing more and more beer, cider, vodka or whatever else I was drinking to achieve that 'blotting out effect' and quickly found myself in that downward spiral of alcohol abuse.

MY PROGRESS

A few people are probably surprised I am still alive after my past antics. Anyway, I am and I don't wish to die of alcoholism or any other illness just yet, thank you. Its funny how your priorities can change. At one time I was not particularly bothered about dying soon and almost accepted that it wouldn't be long if I carried on drinking. As I stopped the drinking, new priorities and things I had forgotten about and used to think were important came back. I would start to feel embarrassed about showing myself up and ashamed about arguing and shouting at other people. Although these are quite normal things for most people who are not drinking, for a reformed alcoholic they are a revelation. For the past ten years, I had chemically manufactured my moods, sometimes with devastating results. If I wanted the effect of confidence I could achieve it by merely downing a few cans, this also worked if I wanted to achieve the chemical emotion of tearfulness. This was usually achieved through vodka or Gin. The problem was, it didn't last very long or I miscalculated and the emotion carried on too long. This was O.K. to a certain extent if I was on my own but not if I was in public. At something like a wedding reception or other occasions when you were obliged to feel happy, I would go over the top and drink the whole bottle of vodka just to make damn sure the happiness would last. It didn't of course and very soon I was telling silly jokes, tripping up on none existent curbs and generally making a prat of myself. It often got worse and I would find myself stuck in the bogs with a bloke I hardly knew.

"ye don't seem to understand, its like an elephant in no clothes"

Luckily, even I didn't fully understand what I was talking about! Out of the toilets I would go, covered in self inflicted urine and my flies still down. The arguments would start once people realised I was pissed, and I craved for attention.

Priorities were not cars and houses and how much money I was earning…………….. No. I was interested in my kids again and my partner Maureen. Don't get me wrong, life didn't become a bag of laughs over night, but just remembering things like what had gone on the day before was a revelation to me. Also feeling "normal" instead of hung-over permanently felt good. Touch wood, these priorities have remained with me and will continue to do so. My memory improves more and more everyday and I do not have the mood swings which I used to have. My improvement is mainly due to abstaining from alcohol. I do not crave alcohol anymore and do not equate it to "having a good time". On the contrary, I see it as a bad feeling and one I do not want to return to.

I try and keep busy most of the time either with my writing, studying or counselling. Life isn't that bad without the drink and I do not constantly have to fight it anymore. Well, that's my report on myself, hopefully I can repeat the process in another years time with the same amount of honesty.

PEOPLE I HAVE MET

I do not want to name the people in person who I talk about in this bit, you will just have to believe me! Sorry.

It goes without saying, that drinkers come from all walks of life, and it can affect them when they are young and when they are old. I have visited many of these people either alone or with my partner for counselling sessions. I have also met people as a fellow drinker and at the time never thought that I would write about them at a later date. I have sat drinking and puking on many park benches in the Huddersfield area. Inadvertently, this has allowed me to write about the people and their feelings and views without having to rely on the textbook method of writing, which I am sure happens.

Its funny how people regard those woman and blokes you see on park benches as 'the rock bottom' of alcoholism. They are the people who have no further to drop on the road to becoming an alcoholic. Or so people tell me, when I have visited them. They will often begin conversations with the immortal words 'I'm not an alcoholic' and often go on to say they don't want to end up on a park bench somewhere. It is as though they like to, or need to see themselves as detached from such events.

'don't think I just sit on a park bench with a bottle of Diamond White in my hands all day and a mucky coat tied together with a piece of string'.

The thing is, a lot of the people I have met have actually been in a worse position. O.K. they may appear alright with half decent clothes on and their bottle of whatever hidden away in a cupboard, but they often drink alone and are ashamed of this fact. Others cling onto their jobs, narrowly escaping dismissal by throwing a 'sicky' once in a while with their employers apparently oblivious to their drinking habits. However, one or two slip ups in the future and they could be sat on a park bench as well.

People on park benches often have a better deal than you think. I admit they tend to drink White Lightening or a few cans of Special Brew, but at least they are honest and have a group of people around them talking to them. I have met many such people when I was drunk and sometimes not as drunk and just in need of someone to talk to. On the whole they are good people and have almost an unwritten code of passing there drink around the group who are sat with them. No body asks too many questions, and the people prefer to keep their private pasts to themselves, a bit like everybody else really. 'Bench drinkers' are not particularly aggressive and only really get noisy when they are blathered. Many of them have strict routines and habits they follow, like who they sit by on the bench and how far on it they sit and what, how and when they are going to get their sandwiches. I once sat next to a bloke on a bench outside Huddersfield bus station. He was covered in bruises around his head area, 'What's happened there?' I asked.

'Just some young kids' he replied, as he watched in case the police moved him on.

The kids had basically bricked him from a distance, as he had just sat there minding his own business. This is the world you live in on the streets as a drinker. He had almost accepted his lot, like the Gin drinkers in Gin Lane, London, who accepted that their young babies in arms may on occasions fall to their deaths in the gutter below.

Dinner time drinkers are another breed apart from park bench drinkers, and I do not mean the type of bloke who just nips in for a quiet half, and then sets off again to meet his wife in the middle of town. I mean the drinker who thinks nothing of supping ten pints each dinner time going for a sleep then back for another session in the evening. This type of dinnertime drinker prefers to be alone and doesn't usually hold out too much conversation. On occasions, the dinnertime drinker will get fired up and argue with anybody who is willing to listen to him, I think you will realise the type of person I am talking about.

Most of the drinkers I have met have some sort of underlying reason they wish to tell me for why they now drink so much.

'I had a good job and lost it five years ago'

'she left me and fleeced me with the divorce'
'I just get so depressed without a drink'

These are all comments made by people I can recall.

My next question which can stop people in their tracks is simply:
'did the drinking start before or after you lost your job or got divorced or depressed?'
After a few sessions I usually get the feeling that the drinking had started well before any divorce e.t.c. and it was always a 'cart before the horse' type situation.

Very few people admit to actually enjoying the drink, and that was why they had landed up with a problem. People can spend weeks trying to convince you they are O.K. and don't drink half as much as they used to do. Why are they bothered about whether we feel they are doing well or not?, Surely they should be thinking, sod off, I am not trying to convince you I'm doing this for myself. People need to use their counselling sessions for their own benefit which means not lying, and taking responsibility for their own recovery. We can only act as reflective sounding boards.

STAYING ON THE WAGON

For many of the people I have seen over the last year, they have had one major problem, and that's staying off the alcohol. People can often last a few days, a week perhaps, but then it takes a grip again and they just cant stop themselves from having another drink. Even after weeks of detox the slightest problem or just an excuse to drink again and they will take it, sometimes big style. Unfortunately, not drinking means NOT DRINKING and this is for the rest of your life. Coming to terms with this notion is not easy and it is like watching a tap dripping for ever more, sometimes. However, it has been done by some and hopefully I will become one of them. It takes about five years of abstinence before you can begin to say you are well on your way. Some people have told me they have no intention to stop completely but will cut down to an acceptable level. That's OK if they really can, but they are a better man than me if they do it. No, I'm afraid I will have to cope with orange juice for evermore, and have hung up my tankard for the last time. One way of coping is, like a said earlier in the book, don't put yourself in situations where it could encourage you to drink. Personally, I cannot cope too well with barbeques and pub situations and others have told me the same. Pubs and barbeques don't give me the same buzz as they used to do, throwing those sausages up in the air whilst very quickly guzzling down some warm and weak larger whenever I got the chance. Or sitting in a pub talking absolute shite to somebody I hardly new. Now these situations bore me rather than fill me with excitement like they used to do. Sorry, but that's the way that it is!

I talked to a bloke last week who with great pride, told me how he had managed to be the sober driver for the night at his works do. He was O.K. until the last couple of hours when the boredom set in and he knew he couldn't have a drink, but he managed.

I feel you have to be constantly aware and vigilant to the possibility of drinking again even if you have managed to abstain for some time. If you are just cutting down, make sure your drinking doesn't reach a level where you could be vulnerable to alcohol, dependence. One way of doing this is to try and make sure that you spend time practising abstaining from alcohol intake. Start off keeping off the alcohol for one day a week then gradually build up until you are achieving four days a week. At this stage, it is within your grasp to stop completely and it is your emotional state which is dictating whether you take the decision to stop completely or carry on drinking. Many people tell you that they need the drink 'for physical withdrawal reasons' whilst lowering their head in almost 'pretend shame'. What a load of bollocks, especially when they have been on some sort of detox programme for nearly a year. They are not physically addicted or suffering any physical withdrawal effects after this length of time. It is emotionally and psychologically that things are not fully right. The alcoholic is so used to drinking, that they find it virtually impossible to give up their routine of drinking every night. This is where the techniques of almost shear willpower need to kick in, amongst other things. The other things include not giving your self as many choices in certain situations. Don't just sit in your local, rejecting all the drinks you are offered by others or just drinking halves.

Don't go to the pub in the first place! Then you don't have to constantly make a decision about what to do with yourself next. You have narrowed it down to just one decision you have to make, going to the pub or not. Unfortunately, off licences bugger this theory up somewhat. Many people turn up at the local off licence night after night at virtually the same time each night. Usually just before closing time the crowd begins to grow.

'Twenty Benson and Hedges and a small box of matches please'

'Oh, and whilst your there, a bottle of THAT please, no, no no!' the bigger one'.
Off you go with your plastic bag, with another night of failure to look forward to.

Really, when I think about it, it is very little to do with willpower, and much more to do with anticipating what you will do in certain situations. If that bottle is available, do you honestly believe you will have the willpower to stop yourself drinking it? Don't go for the bottle in the first place, and don't give yourself the time and money to run out and get it at the last minute. It may be a drastic move to make, but stick to it!

THE EFFECTS ON THE FAMILY

Its more important day by day to realise the effects your drinking has had on your family. I have already written about my break ups and the effect it has had on family members and of course the let downs I have caused in general, but what about others? I have been to see many families and been troubled by the results. Many mothers have over protected their sons and daughters and been unwilling to tell me the whole picture of their siblings drinking. Sometimes, it has taken weeks of talking to find out who the hell has got the problem in the first place. Has the mother been too soft? or have they carried on plying their son with lager just to keep him happy. Where was the father whilst all this was going on?

'Something needs to be done, I'm getting sick of it' said one father.

'He's going to throw him out ye know' replied his mother.

Good! I thought.

The next week what had happened?

There sat the bespectacled geek in his thirties still throwing his threats of leaving home at me. He had just about got round to reading his housing benefit form and realised that he needed a microwave for his new fictitious flat.

His mother tried desperately to please everybody. The new 'sterner' stance for her husband, the compassionate looks for her son and the 'I will do anything that pleases' look for myself and Maureen. Of course nothing happened.

The lad continued to manipulate the situation, and knew his mother would eventually relent and take his side of the discussion.

Why do mothers and fathers do this? Because they love their kids and don't want them to end up in even deeper shit than they are already in.

Unfortunately, they often handle things badly and cannot carry out in practice the things they intended and agreed to do. Instead they use the old 'knee jerk reaction' technique,

'I have thrown his Special Brew down the sink'

Probably not the wisest move you could have made, particularly since you bought it in the first place!
or 'I don't care anymore I'm kicking him out',

This is a bit rich when you have made his meals everyday and cushioned his every move, bar wiping his arse for him.

In short, the family members of a person with a drink problem have all to contribute to the persons recovery and everyday handling.

It was no use with the mother mentioned above, perpetually worrying about her son, with her husband hiding in the shed every time I went to talk to them all.
Consistency is vital in the families approach to a drinker. It is no use one relative saying one thing and another saying something quite different. As a family, people have to realise that the alcoholic

will play one person against another all the time. Their goal is to get that drink down their necks and they will, as I should know, manipulate anybody who stands in their way or they see as a weak link to achieve it.

When subjects such as liver function tests are asked about, the alcoholic will more often than not make any excuse not to have one done.

'I will go in a couple of months when I have fully stopped drinking. If I go to the doctors now and the results are bad, it will only put me off going again'

What they really mean, is, they are scared of having to completely stop drinking and not because they are scared their results might be so bad already.

Families have a tendency to hide things from one another.

'He's been drinking all week, but don't tell his father'

Often you can be put into almost an impossible situation, trying to deal with the problem, whilst not giving away a piece of information you have been entrusted with.

It is so important that families begin to realise when they are being counselled, that this is where they need to put all their cards on the table and stop buggering about with half truths and sometimes down right lies. The thing is, I've heard it all before and it isn't fooling anyone except themselves.

I often ask people to complete a diary of events, and wish that it had been possible for my mum and partner to have kept a video diary of me, particularly when I was at the worst phase of my drinking and then look at when I began to feel better. A video of this sort, would be an invaluable reminder of my antics at the time. I have talked to people obviously, but it is not enough to always drive it home about how bad you really were at the time. Human nature tells us to siphon out the things that go well and are positive, and to forget the times we are arguing with our neighbours whilst pissing up their garden walls or fighting with our partners.

We need our families to survive mentally and physically and they need us to do the same.

DEATH

I have always been a bit scared of dying, which may sound a bit rich coming from me. He, who almost beckoned death into his world with drink. When I look at the dangers I put myself in through no fault of anyone else but me, I can only cringe. When we visit people now, I see people with the same problems as myself everyday, and like me, they still refuse to admit to themselves that they are killing themselves. Some people I have known have actually died. Like the bloke I met whilst I was full throng with my own drinking and stumbled across him in a local pub. He had turned into the opposite type of personality because of his drinking, compared with most people I have known. Rather than turning into a lean and mean and moody bloke who had drunk too much, this bloke just went fat with the drink and very sluggish. He always had been a big drinker ever since we were at school. He left at sixteen and went ino the army. The army must not have done him that much good, but that's the Falklands for ye. He drunk a lot before he went in the army, and increased his intake when he came out. When

I saw him again about ten years later, he had got so big and I mean BIG I did not recognise him at first, even though I had stood next to him for about fifteen minutes at the bar of only a small pub. I had asked him, how he was doing, to which he replied, "nowt, now I've finished in the army, there all bastards ye know"

We walked out into the car park after another few and having rectified the whole world on the way, we met his cheeky and nonchalant daughter there. She swore and abused her dad, verbally. She handed over another bottle of whisky which he took with great speed. I said so long and never saw him again. I was told that he had died about six months later of liver damage, a problem which takes out a lot of drinkers, as you now probably know.

Death is a shit thing whatever the circumstances, unless you die laughing at some funny joke when you are one hundred and ten.....but I digress.

This next chapter was written by my daughter Lydia, shortly before the book was sent for proof reading. Lydia is now twelve years old and getting more mature by the day. I felt it was helpful for her and certainly for me to get her feelings down in writing before she has chance to fully forget those years I spent drunk and totally incapable.

MY DAD AND HOW I NOW FEEL

When I think about how my dad used to be and how he is now, I can see a huge difference in his personality.

I remember the weekends when my mum used to take me and my brother to my dad's house, and I would be so scared to even ring the bell.

What would he do this time? Would he be lying on the floor with sick and his dog's pee surrounding him?

Some weekends, me and my brother had to get up really early and take Max for a walk, otherwise he would just be peeing all over the place and we would be left to clear it up while dad laid on his bed feeling sorry for himself. Other weekends, we had to get up and walk to town with dad. That was the kind of weekend I dreaded the most. He would start off alright, walking to town wasn't that much of a problem, but when we got there dad would go down an alley somewhere and puke. I remember one time when a taxi driver came out of his taxi office and asked if we were ok. I nodded, but he told us to come inside for a cup of tea to calm dad down. He ended up giving us a lift back to dad's flat and the drinking started again.

There's one particular weekend I remember the most. It was on dad's birthday and there was some sort of celebration going on at Greenhead Park. Dad got an idea in his head to walk all the way over there and because me and my brother were the only people dad had to spend his birthday with, we did what he said.

We walked for ages past the University, until we heard fireworks coming from Greenhead Park. Dad fell on the floor crying and shouting; "your not gonna shoot me! I'm better than any of you." Me and my brother looked at each other and frowned for a moment, then realized dad thought he was at war or something weird like that, and he thought the fireworks were guns trying to shoot him.

After about 15 minutes of trying to persuade him to come back home, he finally agreed and we had to literally drag him back to his flat.

These horrible weekends had gone on for so long and since his partner, Susan had left him to go and get married to someone else, we had nobody to help look after dad when we were at school on weekdays…

Until dad met Maureen.

We were at dad's house one weekend, and I think he had made a bit of an effort because someone was coming to visit. When I say he made an effort, I mean he managed to get dressed instead of roaming around in his underpants.

As soon as I met Maureen, I knew she was a nice, kind lady. Mainly because she bought me and my brother an Easter egg and she actually cared about us having a proper tea, eating plenty of fruit and vegetables and making sure we got to bed when we should.

When we were with Maureen, the weekends weren't so bad. She would take us all out for a picnic or take us shopping. We even got to go and see grandma Margaret more often because Maureen had a car and we could go out places. The only problem was, she didn't even know dad had a drinking problem, which was pretty easy to detect. If she had a glass of wine, dad would ask her if he could have one, and he got one. ☹

Maureen didn't even find out he was an alcoholic until dad's best friend told her. Surprisingly, she didn't leave like Susan did. She gave dad support and helped him to get better.
This made me and my brother so much happier, dad had someone to look after him and make sure he didn't drink when we were at school.

Of course, it wasn't that simple and dad has written all about his blips. They went on for ages and we all knew he would never be like he used to be, ever.

Dad and Maureen bought a house together and since then, me and my brother have enjoyed going to stay with them on weekends. Some times he has been perfectly normal and sober, and other times he has been drunk and swearing at us. Either way though, we loved him, and so did Maureen.

Now dad hasn't been drinking for about a year and he has become the dad he used to be.

He has started his counselling and writing his books and not long ago, dad and Maureen took us on holiday to Center Parcs.

I like the person dad is now much more than when he was drinking. I know he will always be an alcoholic but I am proud of him for not drinking for so long.

Thank you Maureen, for supporting him, and letting me and my brother have a normal dad.

Lydia

June 2006

KIDS AND THE EFFECTS OF ALCOHOL

This chapter looks at the problems of children, living with, or at least having regular contact with a problem drinking mum or dad like myself. It deals with hopefully, what the kids endure and the effects it can have on them growing up. As you can guess it was the hardest chapter for me to write, but I only have myself to blame.

I don't need people to tell me for ever more the part drinking can play on troubled families and that the negative consequences of problem drinking extend well beyond the drinker themselves.

- In spite of the drinker's many attempts to hide the fact that they are drinking, children from a very young age are aware of it, and can explain it in terms of their own stress. The child thankfully doesn't blame themselves for their parent's drinking.

- Children make it very clear from a young age how much they dislike their parent's drinking and try and find ways of telling their mum or dad or both, how they feel. My daughter did this in the numerous letters she sent me. They express worry, anger, fear and most hurtful of all, sadness about it. The alcoholic is still their dad or mum, but things have changed. They are not that person they could rely on to get them safely down the motorway on holiday, or to turn up at their school open evening sober and on time.

- It is reported by the media and in fact, by a lot of people I have met over the years that the most serious and common problems concerned drunken violence. Quite naturally it goes without saying that children are very distressed and often frightened by constant arguments about what seems to be anything and everything and physical outbursts, sometimes sadly, directed at them. Even in more sober moments the drunken person has often forgotten what has happened, and the emotional and physical damage is already done.
- Indirect effects are very disruptive often when people have lost their jobs, the police are knocking at your door or your parents are leaving.

- Continued drinking over years can lead to a loss of respect and trust for a long time even when the drinking has stopped. However this respect can be regained through time.
- A lot of families want to, and do try and keep the drink troubles away from outsiders and it is not discussed amongst the wider family. One person I used to see for counselling at his home would be talking to me for an hour in the conservatory of the house, whilst his father went and sat in the shed until the 'ordeal' was over. It was 'nothing to do with him'
- Sadly, its too late for me to just gradually introduce my kids to the damaging effects of alcohol, my son is fifteen next time and will make his own decisions. By the time your child is a teenager, he or she should be very familiar with the facts about alcohol. I have to be as open and honest about the subject as possible, which I don't think is a bad thing, given my circumstances. During my son's and daughter's future teenage years, it is almost inevitable that they are more than likely to engage in risky behaviour. As they strive for more independence and hang out with their

mates, they may have a go at defying others wishes or advice. Kids like and need to be liked by their mates and peer group, therefore they will copy them to a certain extent. The only thing you can do is guide and gain their trust. Preaching, punishing and giving threats will just reinforce their views of you as a boring old fart who they don't want to be like.

• Despite your efforts, your child may still use and abuse alcohol. The warning signs are just the same as with everyone else:

- the smell of the alcohol
- sudden changes in mood or attitude
- change in attendance or performance at school
- loss of interest in school, sports, or other activities
- discipline problems at school
- withdrawal from family and friends
- secrecy
- association with a new group of mates, who they are hell bent from stopping you meeting them.
- the classic, alcohol disappearing from your drinks cabinet. Luckily, there is not much chance of this one happening to me!
- depression and a general sulkiness

Obviously, don't go into a permanent panic, that any of these things in isolation mean your kids have suddenly changed into an alcoholic, just be aware that they could be warning signs. Growing into an adult is a time of change, physically, socially and in the way they think and view life in general. This can lead at best to erratic behaviour and mood swings as kids try to cope with all these changes. Remember when you started to get bum fluff on your chin or you worried that you were the only one who hadn't had sex in your class, or perhaps that was just me! If your child is beginning to go overboard with the drink, there will usually be a number of signs, like suddenly changing friends, the way they dress their behaviour, attitude, mood and other such things. Personally, I started wearing very high 'platform' shoes and smoking in the vain hope that I could get served in a pub!

Try and keep things in perspective, and don't jump to conclusions too readily, you could be in danger of making them rebel against you even more. Listen to what they have to say and show them that you want to take an interest in the things they do.

SOME POEMS
and
STORIES TO FINISH

DRINK

What do you think?
Long moments of nothingness,
Long moments of emptiness,
Long moments of desperation,
Long moments of contemplation.

What do you feel?
Feelings of sadness,
Feelings of unwanted ness,
Feelings of helplessness,
Wanting it to end.

ALCOHOL

ANGRY WITH IT
LETHARGY BECAUSE OF IT
CAN'T COPE WITH IT
OBSESSED WITH IT
HATE IT
OVER POWERED BY IT
LYING FOR IT

WHAT CAN I DO ABOUT IT?

CAROLYN

Each day is a struggle just to
keep the drink at bay,
Do I really need the drink to
get me through the day?

Its all around me and temptation
is never far away,
Do I not go to the supermarket
just in case I should stray?

Do I alienate myself from friends who
have asked me to go to the pub today…?
And if I wasn't drinking what would I say?

What happens when a week has passed
and I forget that hangover feel,
How can I learn to press on and
this time give up (drinking) for real?

You see this is where I'm at…..
a crossroads I feel,
Do I choose health and sobriety
and get a better deal?

Life is an uphill struggle at times
and I thought alcohol was the way,
But I only found that by drinking
the hill gets bigger by the day.

I'm happily married
with three young children.......

So why does alcohol play such a factor in my life?

In January this year I resolved to get my liver function tests better than they were at present......
Therefore the drink went for six weeks.....I was happier than I had been for some time and certainly felt more in control. I had the tests, which were greatly improved and then of course..........
the 'just one drink won't hurt' feeling came over me.

By mid February, I was back to drinking a bottle to a bottle and a half of wine a day, usually in the evenings, when I could pull on the curtains in front of a nice warm fire (and only my husband and myself was aware of how often and how much I was drinking). I know that this amount may not be a lot, by some peoples standards, but to me the fact that I was drinking everyday and my 'weekly units' were nearer a hundred a week rather than the fourteen units they should be, then it's time to take action.

It was February this year that I read Gary Westwell's article in the Examiner……..

In early March I contacted Gary. I guess contacting someone who understood the 'vicious circle' effect that alcohol can have on your life was a relief. I finally felt there was some hope, I was certainly tired of the direction my life was taking at that time. I also realised the only person who could change things for the better was me. It was March already, three months into the year and apart from walking the dogs and doing stuff for the kids, I rarely went out on public transport and particularly not on my own.

I had several counselling sessions with Gary, but more often I found it easier to communicate by e-mail…..probably for me, it felt safer and easier to put across how I was feeling at the time. At one of these sessions, Gary mentioned the 'Lifeline Way Ahead' and 'Outlook' projects. I arranged an appointment to go there, but its easy to get a vision in your head of what to expect…….I was pleasantly surprised. The staff were very friendly and helpful, they really were interested in me.

I did attend the alcohol course they provided…..
Which yes, gave me all the facts about alcohol
and the harm it was doing….but certainly I didn't
get any willpower to stop drinking from it.

I certainly wanted to get healthier and it was
suggested I try the gym…Oh my god! I
thought….. Thinking of 'size 10 ladies and good
looking men with muscles…again this was just a
preconceived idea and I have now been going for
the last two months! (My husband has also
recently joined the gym too). I also attended the
outdoor sessions at 'Outlook'…..walking,
cycling, climbing etc and hope to do plenty more
of these activities in the near future. I have also
attended a first aid course there.

I can't profess that I have beaten the alcohol, far
from it…….and the weekends are usually the
hardest. For example, on Saturday night I had a
bottle and a half and woke up with a hangover on
Sunday morning and the usual resolve, to not 'go
there again'…….this lasted until eight o'clock on
Sunday evening, when I gave in to yet another
bottle of wine. As for tonight, we will see?

It's easy for me to feel in control during the day, but when the 'eight o'clock' syndrome comes…. I'm really desperate for that drink.

Carolyn

Well that's the evils of drink for you in a nutshell! You know the pitfalls, illness, low moods, irritation and anger about your plight, but still you end up drinking, sometimes until it is too late to recover anything. Lets hope it is not you!

Notes and comments

Notes and comments

Notes and comments

Some helpful addresses

Addiction - rehabilitation and treatment

Before I re-write this particular section to some extent I must apologise for missing out an organisation who have helped me a lot over the years and which I still attend some of their meetings when I am not counselling or taking the kids swimming e.t.c. The group I have attended is the first on the list. This is in case I forgot and got another telling off from one of their chairs! Seriously, thanks a lot for your help and support.

- ## Kirklees Alcohol Advisory Service Ltd. (K.A.S.S.)

This group offers a drop in centre at The Methodist Mission in Huddersfield town centre on a Wednesday between 7.00p.m. and 9.00p.m. The sessions are for both men and woman and include and encourage carers to attend and contribute. The admission is free and tea and coffee is available. You can speak if you want to but are not pressured to do so. There is also a (K.A.S.S.)

Ladies Only Group held on a Monday at the Salvation Army Building, Prospect Street, Huddersfield.

• __Lifeline Way Ahead Alcohol Service__

Way ahead is an open access confidential service which is client centred and is Lifelines first point of contact for all individuals affected by substance use in Kirklees. Workers will support progress with the individual via a range of engagement techniques beginning with a holistic assessment identifying their needs. Individuals will be supported to look at options available and what they can expect from these options and the service. Way ahead will invite individuals to attend a four week group session that will look at coping techniques, cutting down, safe limits and then further support if required. Lifeline also has a range of other services that will support individuals to look at confidence building, health and fitness, employment and education and work with an individual's readiness to develop new social environments that don't include alcohol.

If you are experiencing difficulties with Alcohol then contact us on 01484 353333 or 01924 438383

Alternatively, you can just drop into one of our services for immediate advice and information: 12 Station Street,Huddersfield, HD1 1LZ

- **Alcoholics Anonymous-** the only requirement for A.A. membership is a desire to stop drinking. There are no fees for attending. It is not attached to any sect, denomination, politics, organisation or institution.

- **Alcohol Concern-** this is a national agency on alcohol misuse. They work to reduce the incidence of alcohol related harm and to increase the range and quality of services available to people with problems. They offer fact sheets and other publications. www.alcoholconcern.org.uk

- **Al-Anon-** Al-Anon (which includes Alateen for younger people has been offering help to families and friends for over 50 years.

They believe that it is a family disease and that each alcoholic affects the lives of at least four other people. They will see people whatever their relationship is with the alcoholic.

- **•** **www.detoxplus.co.uk-** **called PIERPOINT** they offer a + 12 step abstinence based treatment for alcohol, heroin, cocaine and benzos. They provide female focus treatment exclusively for woman and have an addiction treatment centre based at 385 Clifton Dr North, St Anne's on Sea FY8 2NW. There goal is to provide people with help with substance abuse, dependency or addiction.
- CALL 0845 458 3700

- **•** **www.cdcgisburne.com** - **called COVENENT DEPENDENCY CENTRE** they offer detoxification from alcohol and drugs with a free assessment and in-patient programme. Based at Abbey Gisburne Park Hospital, Gisburne, Lancashire BB7 4XH. They provide a telephone advice line, group and individual therapy, family therapy after care care and day care programme. People may be referred privately or through the N.H.S. and there is no catchment area as such.

- CALL 01200 445693

- **<u>PRIORY CLINIC NOTTINGHAM -</u>** Offer treatment for additions including drugs and alcohol. They are based at Ransom Road, Nottingham, NG3 5GS.Founded in 1990, it is a 18 bedded unit providing residential and day care services to help individuals and families to recover from the physical and emotional effects of alcohol and drug problems and to achieve healthy and productive lives. It is a free standing facility, specialising in working with the N.H.S. and statutory providers. They also accept self funded patients and patients covered by private medical insurance. Private psychiatric appointments are available on an outpatient basis. To access the service initial contact can be made directly to the clinic by the patient, relative friend or professional organisation who will then be given information about referral, assessment admission proceedings and funding. A free assessment interview is available to establish care needs and the likely costs. The Clinic is open 24 hours a day, 365 days a year for residential treatment. Assessment by appointment only. Information line available 24 hours a day- Free Addiction Line: 0845 60 50 121

- CALL 0115 969 3388

- ## **Turning Point**
- they are based at 24 Apple House Trinity Church Gate in Wakefield. They offer counselling, advice, information and support to current or former substance users, their families and friends. The project actively seeks to reduce the health risks associated with drinking and drug use.

The service is for anyone in the Wakefield and District areas who are concerned about their own or another's alcohol or drug use, whether the drugs are ellicit or prescribed (e.g. Tranquillizers). Referrals can come from any source and drop-in visits are welcome. The project has three office bases one situated in Wakefield city centre, one in Hemworth and one in Castleford. Please contact each team for drop- in times and details of referral procedures.

- CALL 01924 377704

- • **www.cygehealth.co.uk**

deal with people with alcohol problems with in-patient treatment and a 12 day detox and therapy programme.

- CALL 0845 070 4166

- **'Womenspace'**

This is a professional service which has been established for over twenty years. It uses a confidential appointments system and is predominantly for woman due to the nature of the issues they deal with. The staff are professionally trained, qualified and experience counsellors with membership of the British Association for Counselling. They have adopted strict levels of confidentiality. They cover all issues connected to woman and offer a quiet, warm and comfortable setting for their activities. They will also pass on referrals to myself at Empathy support services if you want them to.

- CALL 01484 536272

- ## **Empathy support services**

This is an organisation set up by myself and my wife following the response we received for my first book. Initially we wanted to spread the word and educate people about drink problems through producing books and general literature. This book is published by empathy support services. We have also expanded and now offer advice, counselling and support both on an individual basis and for groups. We now have a web site, telephone advice line and an e-mail service. We will visit people at home and also use the offices based at 'Womenspace' 51 Estate Buildings, Railway Street, Huddersfield. We can be contacted on 01484 469030 or through 'Womenspace' 01484 536272.

Please remember this is not a definitive list of all the people who can help you. It would have been useful to me living in the Huddersfield area. If you are a relative or friend of a person with a drink problem it is useful to have some addresses at hand in case you end up with an emergency admission on your hands. Remember you can sometimes be desperate and need a reliable telephone number of someone who you can trust and understand and not tell you it will be a week before you can receive a service.

There are many other privately run counselling services, local N.H.S. and Social Services who you can ring in your local area. Always check first to see who is reputable with G.P.s etc to ensure you can receive the service which will meet your needs.

Well that's it for now if you have any comments or ideas for another piece of work that could help someone with a drink related problem please give me a ring on **01484 469030**

Gary
1st November 2006